LEADING WITH
HEART
& SOUL

LESSONS FROM A LIFETIME IN LEADERSHIP

DAVE COLE
WITH KEITH WALL

ILLUMIFY
MEDIA.COM

Leading with Heart and Soul

All Scripture quotations, unless otherwise indicated, are taken from the Holy Bible, New International Version®, NIV®. Copyright ©1973, 1978, 1984, 2011 by Biblica, Inc.™ Used by permission of Zondervan. All rights reserved worldwide, www.zondervan.com. The "NIV" and "New International Version" are trademarks registered in the United States Patent and Trademark Office by Biblica, Inc.™ Scripture quotations marked (NASB)® taken from the New American Standard Bible®, Copyright © 1960, 1962, 1963, 1968, 1971, 1972, 1973, 1975, 1977, 1995, 2020 by The Lockman Foundation. Used by permission. All rights reserved. (www.lockman.org)

Scriptures marked (NKJV) taken from the New King James Version®. Copyright © 1982 by Thomas Nelson. Used by permission. All rights reserved. Scripture quotations marked (NLT) are taken from the Holy Bible, New Living Translation, copyright ©1996, 2004, 2007, 2013 by Tyndale House Foundation. Used by permission of Tyndale House Publishers, Inc., Carol Stream, Illinois 60188. All rights reserved.

The views and opinions expressed in this book are those of the author and do not necessarily reflect the official policy or position of Illumify Media Global.

Published by

Illumify Media Global

www.IllumifyMedia.com

"Let's bring your book to life!"

Paperback ISBN: 978-1-964251-36-3

Cover design by Debbie Lewis

Printed in the United States of America

*I dedicate this book to my loving and gracious God,
who chose to bless greatly a modestly gifted man like me
and wait patiently until I was ready to have
a true relationship with him.*

*And to my beautiful, caring, and wise wife, Nancy,
the love of my life and my partner on every step
of our journey together.*

Contents

PROLOGUE

Why Me?
Only by the Grace of God

*Leaders grow by learning from challenges
and leaning on God's wisdom.*

My life is the story of how a modestly gifted man achieved significant success in a very difficult and challenging world.

With help from a gracious God.

And help from a wonderful wife.

And help from fabulous friends and colleagues.

When I say I am "a modestly gifted man," that is not false humility or self-deprecating modesty—that's the truth. I don't believe I possess any particular talents or innate traits that would have indicated, at a young age, that I'd go on to be a leader of large teams of people at nation-wide corporations. I don't believe I was endowed with great giftedness that would lead me to enjoy high successes and endure low failures.

What I did have was a God who directed me even when I wasn't looking for his direction and waited patiently for me when I had wandered away from him. I also had people throughout my life who believed in me when I didn't believe in myself and lifted me up when I fell down. And I had a teachable spirit and a sponge-like openness to absorb any drop of wisdom that I lacked.

Over the course of my forty-year career as a corporate leader, I learned something extremely important: Effective leadership is most often forged in the crucible of hard lessons, failure, and difficulty. While successes and achievements shape a leader's career and legacy, it is the setbacks and challenges that provide the deepest learning experiences.

Ultimately, the road to effective leadership is paved with challenges, and it is through these experiences that leaders develop the wisdom, patience, and strength needed to succeed.

I didn't understand these truths until, at age thirty, I read *The Road Less Traveled* by M. Scott Peck. I had been away from parents and family for ten years and had married my loving and beautiful wife, Nancy, eight years prior. At that point in life, I had an outstanding management job with a highly regarded company and looked forward to a great career and life. But I felt a sense that things still could be better. Despite all the wonderful aspects of my life at that time—a healthy income, a fantastic wife, close friends—I couldn't understand why everything didn't seem easier, more fulfilling, and less problematic.

> **Effective leadership is most often forged in the crucible of hard lessons, failure, and difficulty.**

Much of *The Road Less Traveled* centers on the theme that life is difficult, and it is through difficulty that we grow, mature, and learn to love. As Dr. Peck wrote, "It is in the whole process of meeting and solving problems that life has meaning. Problems are the cutting edge that distinguishes between success and failure. Problems call forth our courage and our wisdom; indeed, they create our courage and our wisdom. It is only because of problems that we grow mentally and spiritually. It is through the pain of confronting and resolving problems that we learn."[1]

I came to see that every problem and peril is an opportunity to grow. I am glad I learned this early in my career because leaders are regularly called upon to solve problems, overcome challenges, and turn setbacks into steps forward. With this perspective, I resolved to become the best I could be as a manager and leader—and to help others to be the best they could be.

FORGED BY FIRE

True leadership is not just about knowing how to lead when everything is going smoothly; it's about navigating adversity with resilience, humility, and the willingness to learn from mistakes. The most effective leaders are those who have been tested, who have faced obstacles, made missteps, and emerged stronger and wiser.

Failure teaches leaders lessons that success cannot. When a leader experiences failure—whether it's a project that falls apart, a missed opportunity, or a lapse in judgment—it forces them to reflect on what went wrong. In these moments of introspection, leaders gain clarity about their decision-making processes, their communication skills, and their ability to adapt to unforeseen circumstances. The humility that comes from failure often makes leaders more empathetic, understanding, and effective in guiding their teams through future challenges.

Adversity also builds resilience, a crucial quality for any leader. Difficult times demand perseverance, creativity, and the ability to stay focused on long-term goals, even when the short-term outlook is bleak. Leaders who have faced adversity are often better equipped to handle stress, make decisions under pressure, and inspire confidence in their teams. They understand that setbacks are a natural part of any process and the ability to press forward is what separates great leaders from the rest.

Through hard lessons, failure, and difficulty, leaders learn not only about their own limitations but also about the importance of collaboration and trust. Challenges often highlight the necessity of relying on others—whether it's team members, mentors, or colleagues—to overcome obstacles.

Leaders who have experienced failure, as I have, often develop greater appreciation for the strengths and perspectives of those around them, realizing that leadership is not a solitary endeavor but a collective one. In this way, hardship doesn't just shape individual leaders, but it also strengthens their ability to build cohesive, resilient teams capable of weathering storms together.

GOD WALKS WITH US

I learned another valuable lesson that corresponds with the one I just shared: though our lives are full of difficulties and even disasters, God walks with us through all of them. It took me a long time to understand and rely on this Old Testament promise: "So do not fear, for I am with you; do not be dismayed, for I am your God. I will strengthen you and help you; I will uphold you with my righteous right hand" (Isaiah 41:10). And as Jesus told his followers, "I have told you these things, so that in me you may have peace. In this world you will have trouble. But take heart! I have overcome the world" (John 16:33).

I believe God has a life plan for each of us. I believe this because of what I have seen in my life and in the lives of others. I believe that a life lived with God will be good for each person and good for everyone we connect with over our lifetime. I didn't always believe this, but after I truly got to know God in my fifties, I began to trust him and lean on him.

God used my mistakes and failures to help me turn to him. I had chosen to "go it alone" for many years, because I saw him through the lens of my strict, severe, and fear-driven Catholic church upbringing. I grew up believing I could never, ever please God. I knew of *that* God—the one who is harsh, judgmental, demanding—but not the *real* God, who exudes love, joy, peace, patience, and kindness.

Now more than ever, I believe God guided me through decisions that led to success and walked with me through decisions that led to failure. I also believe God knew I would go into sales and receive outstanding training and experience at Procter and Gamble. God knew I would be transferred to the Milwaukee district, where I would learn a lot, be greatly challenged, and be the key support person for the new executive who would become the top sales executive a P&G.

Most importantly, God knew I would meet the wife he had provided for me, my partner for more than fifty years. Nancy encouraged me every night when I came home with my most recent challenge and always helped me to see the opportunity in the problems I encountered. Her father, a brilliant businessman, became my mentor for forty-six years. There is no question that this is God's work.

WE ARE GOD'S CRAFTSMANSHIP

God's plan for each person is a masterful design, crafted with care and intention. This certainly includes young, humble businesspeople who are being shaped into leaders of excellence. This journey is one of transformation, where each experience, whether triumph or trial, serves a purpose in molding one's character and leadership style.

For those at the beginning of their careers, the business world can seem overwhelming, with its pressures to succeed, meet targets, and outperform competitors. However, within this challenging environment, God is at work, using each situation to build the qualities that define true leadership—qualities like integrity, compassion, humility, and resilience.

In the early stages of their professional journey, young businesspeople often encounter scenarios that test their core values. They might face decisions that require them to balance profitability with ethical considerations, or they may have to navigate office politics where maintaining integrity could cost them favor with influential colleagues.

These moments of tension and difficulty are where God's refining process is most active. Each time they choose the harder right over the easier wrong, they strengthen their moral compass and become more aligned with God's principles. Over time, these small, consistent choices build a foundation of trustworthiness and respect—within their teams, among the broader business community, and in their personal lives.

God also orchestrates relationships and experiences that play crucial roles in the development of young leaders. Mentors—whether found in the workplace, church, or community—provide guidance that is both practical and spiritual. These mentors often share their own experiences of navigating the business world with faith, offering advice that helps young leaders avoid pitfalls and seize opportunities for growth.

As young business professionals progress through career stages, they begin to develop a deeper understanding that their work is a form of stewardship. They realize that their careers are not just about personal achievement, but they are opportunities to serve others and glorify God. This shift in mind-set transforms their approach to leadership. Rather than pursuing success for their own gain, they seek to uplift their teams, make ethical decisions that benefit the community, and use their influence to bring about positive change. They start to see their roles as part of a larger narrative— God's narrative—where every decision and action contributes to a greater good.

> God's plan for each person is a masterful design, crafted with care and intention.

As growing leaders continue to follow God's guidance, they are gradually transformed into leaders of excellence. They are not just effective in their roles but also respected and admired for their integrity, empathy, and vision. They understand that their success is measured not by wealth or status but by their faithfulness to God's calling and their ability to make a positive difference in the lives of others.

Ultimately, their journey is a powerful testimony to the transformative power of faith in the business world. As they lead with humility, wisdom, and a servant's heart, they inspire others to see the workplace as a mission field where God's love and justice can be demonstrated. Their example encourages others to seek God's purpose for their own lives, fostering a generation of leaders who are committed not just to business excellence but to making the world a better place. In doing so, they fulfill the unique plan that God has for them, becoming leaders who not only achieve success but also leave a lasting legacy of faith and integrity.

In the pages that follow, I offer a brief "travelogue" through my formative years, learning years, and leadership years. Part One of this book demonstrates how a hardworking but modestly gifted kid can grow up to be a hardworking but modestly gifted leader of corporations and organizations. My hope is that my story inspires young leaders (and everyone) to maximize their potential and fully use their God-given talents, no matter their background or beginnings.

Part Two of this book is my humble offering of effective leadership strategies—practical principles mostly learned the hard way by me. Emerging leaders might view these as tools in their toolbox that can be used to build their own unique leadership style and guide their teams toward greatness. Seasoned leaders might find my ideas to be helpful reminders of their own lessons learned, with perhaps fresh ideas and inspiration to continue growing into ever more effective leaders.

Most of all, throughout these pages you will see how God can inspire all kinds of people—including you and me—to become faithful and faith-filled leaders, accomplish his purposes, and change the world for the better.

Part One

Every Good Thing in My Life Came from God

1

A Firm Foundation of Faith

*God knew exactly the parents and family
I should have.*

We all make thousands of choices throughout our lives that will determine our life trajectory. But one of the most vital and decisive factors in our lives we have no control over whatsoever.

I am referring to the family we are born into. None of us can choose who our parents will be, who our siblings will be, or the places where we'll grow up.

But still, our parents, siblings, extended families, and communities shape us, steer us, and shepherd us in myriad ways. For all of us, our early years largely determine who we will become in all the years that follow. This is why I am thankful to God every day for placing me in the family he chose for me.

I was born to wonderful parents in Toledo, Ohio, two years after World War II ended. My mother, Marjorie, was a woman of great faith who prayed every day during the war that God would safely bring home her husband, Bob, a staff sergeant squad leader in General Patton's Fourth Armored Division and her brother, my uncle Bob, who was a navigator in the Eighth Air Force Division. Thanks to the prayers of my mother and grandmother, both my father and uncle returned home alive.

Financially, we weren't rich by any measure. In fact, it's accurate to say that our family lived week to week, paycheck to paycheck, and sometimes hand to mouth. My dad worked as a cabinet maker. When Dad brought home his weekly paycheck, he and Mom would allocate varying amounts of it for the mortgage, food, gas, and other essential expenses, allowing very little for extras. I'm sure many people considered us "poor," but we never considered ourselves that way. We had a family culture that appreciated every dollar, worked hard for every dollar, and stretched every dollar. Those were valuable skills and perspectives for a lad (me) who would one day become a leader and corporate executive.

> **For all of us, our early years largely determine who we will become in all the years that follow.**

What our family lacked in money and material possessions we more than made up for by parents who enriched their seven children in more meaningful ways. The values taught by our parents were exceptional and full of potent life lessons. We were taught to be grateful for every blessing God provided, keep our word no matter what, tell the truth in every circumstance, and respect all people at all times. We were taught to "love your neighbor," and we tried diligently to do this.

Despite our efforts, though, our neighbors not only didn't love us but looked down on us. You might say they considered us "trailer trash" unfit to live in their neighborhood. In fact, I can't remember any neighbor, in the fourteen years that I lived in my childhood house, saying hi or even saying anything to any of us. It was clear to me they felt our family didn't belong in their neighborhood, and it made me angry that they thought so lowly of us.

The neighbors' superior attitude, however, did cause me to work even harder as I shoveled snow or mowed lawns, trying to earn money for a proper barbershop haircut (my dad did most of our haircuts). Being looked down on as a child also taught me a valuable lesson for my years in the business world: never look down on anyone!

My parents didn't seem to let the neighbors' condescending attitude get to them, and they lived their lives demonstrating their Christian values of love, respect, honesty, and hard work. This couldn't have been easy with their brood of rambunctious children and just enough money to get by on much of the time. Our parents were a great gift from God to all of us.

When I was five, my dad saved me. My brother Denny and I were playing with a little red wagon. I decided to walk on the bed of the wagon while it sped toward a fence. Crashing into the wooden planks, I impaled my left arm, and the wound bled profusely. Horrified, my brothers and sisters ran to get my father. He had been taking a bath but jumped out of the tub, threw on some clothes, and hurried outside. Finding me gushing blood, he immediately applied a tourniquet as he had learned to do in the war. Dad rushed me to the hospital, where a surgeon stitched me up.

To this day, decades later, I can still see the five-inch scar on my arm—a reminder of my heavenly Father's protection and earthly father's wisdom. It's not an exaggeration to say I could have bled out and died if not for my dad's calm thinking and quick action. God used my dad's knowledge as a seasoned soldier to save me, as he had saved fellow soldiers during combat.

LEARNING MY LIMITATIONS

As the eldest son, I was chosen at age ten to be Dad's helper on extra jobs in the evening and on weekends. Dad always sought out "side gigs" to provide for our family. He would take on construction work, handyman projects, or any kind of hands-on labor that paid a buck.

Unfortunately, I proved to be completely inept on virtually every project he assigned to me, even with his constant instruction. I continued to do my best at the tasks but with little success. The only way I seemed to excel was cleaning the job site. Not exactly a craftsman-level skill, but I worked hard and tried to please Dad. Fortunately for my dad, I had several other brothers who were much more talented in construction and handyman work.

Most of my life, including high school, I was plagued with sickness and health problems. As a baby, I couldn't tolerate baby formula, and when my mother gave me a bottle, I immediately rejected it. I also had a much more serious problem as a sophomore in high school because I started to pass out. There was concern that I might die. My mother took me to numerous doctors, who examined me and couldn't diagnose the problem. Finally, Mom took me to an allergist, who diagnosed me with an extreme allergy to corn.

The allergist gave me both good news and bad news. The good news was that I wouldn't be able to serve in the armed forces. At that time, the Vietnam War was raging and my draft number for active duty was very low, a sure indication I would be drafted. Although I wanted to fulfill my duty to my country and make my veteran father proud, nobody (including me) wanted to go into combat in Vietnam.

The bad news was that I would never be able to eat or breathe in corn or corn products for the rest of my life, which meant I couldn't go outdoors in areas where corn grew. Since we lived in Northwestern Ohio, where an abundance of corn was grown, outdoor sports and other activities were ruled out for me.

> Being looked down on as a child taught me a valuable lesson for my years in the business world: never look down on anyone!

My dad encouraged all of his children to attend college, as he was a child of the Great Depression and was only able to go to school until the eighth grade since his family needed him to work. After the allergist's report and knowing that my family wouldn't be able to provide any money for college tuition, I decided to create my own life and earn money for college.

The day after I graduated high school, my dad sat me down for a talk.

"Dave," he said, "you know how proud I am of you. And now you are grown up. If you want to continue living in this house, you will need to pay rent."

Some people might have taken offense, as if Dad was being coldhearted and insensitive. I didn't then and I don't now. As always, he was being realistic—he had many mouths to feed and children to provide for. More than that, he was telling me it was time to live as an adult and make my own way in the world. Dad gave me a firm nudge out of the nest, confident he and Mom had given me the values and skills to succeed in life.

2

Open Doors and New Paths

Each opportunity is a chance to learn and grow.

While the most basic point of work is to make money to live, I always viewed each work situation as an opportunity to learn and grow.

Although my first professional job came with Procter and Gamble, I began as an "entrepreneur" when I was twelve years old, mowing lawns, shoveling snow, raking leaves, and doing other odd jobs. Growing up in Toledo, Ohio, where the winters were often harsh, I eagerly awaited storms to dump tons of snow. For me, big snowstorms were a big money-making opportunity.

I remember knocking on the door of our neighbors Mr. and Mrs. Findley in the winter of 1957.

"Good morning, my name is David Cole, and I live down the street," I announced. "I would like to offer my services to shovel this heavy, deep snow from your driveway and sidewalk. I believe you will find me to be reliable and trustworthy."

Right away, Mr. Findley said, "You're hired."

He added that if I did a good job and if I could come early in the morning so he could get to work on time, I could have the job for as long as I wanted it. I never disappointed him and was his "go-to guy" for the next four years, whether it meant shoveling snow, mowing his lawn, raking leaves, or any other job he wanted done. He paid me well, and I learned about customer service from the Findleys, who were my best customers. They told me exactly what they wanted in each job, and I provided my most diligent work. In return, they were generous in the wages they paid me.

> God had given me a great work ethic and a good way with customers— mostly because of the great parents he had given me.

My first real employed job was at our local Kroger grocery store. I had been shopping at the store for years, picking up groceries for our family. One day I approached the store manager and said, "Sir, I would like to work at your store. And so I am asking you for a job."

"Sorry, kid," he replied, "there are no job openings right now. But you can always check back later on."

I came back the next week and asked for a job again. And again, he said he still didn't have any openings. But I kept going back, week after week, politely and respectfully asking for a job.

Finally, the fourth time I asked him for a job, he told me, "Look, son, I am so tired of seeing you and having you pester me for a job that I'm going to give you one. Your job will be to carry out groceries to customers' cars. It can be tedious and tiring—and it's the lowest-paying job at the store. It's yours if you want it."

"You bet I want it!" I told him. "Thank you, sir. I can guarantee that I will be your best employee."

I worked extremely hard, carrying out countless bags of groceries, always with a smile and a kind word to the customers. Plus, I looked for other ways to pitch in and help the other workers. I cheerfully performed all the grunt work no one else wanted to do. In three months, I was named the store's employee of the quarter. The job paid only ten dollars a week, minus union dues and taxes, but I was extremely grateful. God had given me a great work ethic and a good way with customers—mostly because of the great parents he had given me.

LESSONS LEARNED FROM SWEAT AND TOIL

Among the jobs I held while in high school and college included working for the A&P grocery store in their industrial bakery. One of the most challenging parts of the job was unloading the weekly railcars of hefty bags of flour and sugar, an entire day of backbreaking work. I had to walk into the railcar, hoist a hundred-pound bag onto my shoulder, trudge out, and place it on a hand truck. For eight or ten hours straight!

> Because we were required to wear a suit and tie to work every day, I occasionally got side work as a pallbearer and that paid very well—five dollars per funeral!

Other hard work included cleaning up Toledo City Parks, especially in the fall with all the leaves on the ground. We filled truck after truck cleaning up the parks. I earned tuition for my freshman year of college at Toledo Central Catholic High School binding textbooks in the summer and working in the cafeteria during school days.

Next, I sold men's clothing for three years from 1966 to 1969. I got the job because the store manager, Bill Adler, was one of my customers at the Kroger store where I was bagging and carrying out groceries. As I took out groceries to his car one evening, he asked if I would like a better-paying job. I told him I would, and he asked me how much I was paid at Kroger. After I answered, he said he would pay me 50 percent more and give me more hours per week. I accepted the job and worked for the Springer's store on and off for four years during college.

That was a great learning experience dealing with customers, understanding the men's clothing business, and helping customers look their best. In addition, because we were required to wear a suit and tie to work every day, I occasionally got side work as a pallbearer, and that paid very well—five dollars per funeral!

STRUGGLES AS A STUDENT

When I enrolled in Miami University of Ohio, I had the challenge of handling tough courses, feeding myself, and finding a place to live. During the first year, I lived with two fraternity brothers in a tiny apartment, and we each had one meal a day at dinner. It was always fried chicken because we could get it cheap, and to this day I don't like fried chicken. I didn't own a warm jacket, but one of my fraternity brothers lent me a navy peacoat for the whole first winter.

Besides this, I needed money for books. I would save money to go home by hitchhiking the two hundred miles from Miami to Toledo.

In the first term at Miami, from August to late November, I lost thirty pounds, which made my wonderful mother very concerned. Though I had a job with one of the four best restaurants in Miami washing pots and pans, I kept it for only a few weeks. I switched to a better-paying job selling shoes for a dollar an hour with more total hours per week. In late November, though, the shoe store went out of business because the owner hadn't paid his bills.

When the shoe store went out of business, I asked for a job at the Boar's Head Bar across the street. They also paid a dollar an hour but included tips. Unfortunately, I don't think anyone I knew was ever tipped in the four years I worked there, as college kids don't tip. However, if I was hungry, and I always was, I could have a hamburger and a beer for free. Because I worked most nights and wasn't able to study as much as I should have, my GPA wasn't as good as it could've been. Also, I probably lost some hearing because of the loud rock bands.

With a bachelor's degree in hand and a few bucks in my pocket, I was poised to take the next steps on my journey forward.

3

A Steep Learning Curve

First steps into the business world provide valuable lessons.

God guided me and prepared me to land a job with one of the premier companies in the world. But that would require a redirection from my anticipated life plan. With my college education completed in the fall of 1969, I was the proud owner of a bachelor's degree in history and government, with plans to become a high school history teacher.

Early in my college experience, I had considered a career in business. But after I took two business courses, Accounting 101 and Human Resource Management—which I found incredibly boring—I decided that business was probably not my calling. Even so, when it was time to find a job, I put my résumé into both the teaching placement office and, on a whim, in the business placement office. I did this because during my junior year in college my cooperating teacher/mentor at Hamilton Garfield High School, Mr. Kelly, had told me I had talent and recommended I pursue a career in business. Student teaching proved difficult and unfulfilling, and I knew teacher compensation would be only five thousand dollars per year. That was well below what I could earn in the business world.

So, rather than becoming a history teacher, I followed God's lead to pursue a sales job at Procter and Gamble, which at the time was one of the most preferred companies to work for in the world. While finishing my college studies, I was offered three interviews at different firms, including Kawneer, Firestone, and Procter and Gamble. One of the few friends I had at Miami couldn't believe I had an interview with the vaunted P&G, which was a surprise to me too.

Scheduled to be the last person interviewed that day, I arrived at the P&G offices on time and wearing my only suit. The interview team included a district manager, a regional manager, and three unit managers. They were clearly worn out from a long day of interviews. I sensed that if I didn't impress them quickly, they would shortly end the interview and send me on my way. I was right about that because when I was part of this same hiring process a couple of years later, we were instructed to ask a few tough questions right off the bat. If the individual didn't do well, we thanked the candidate for their time and said good-bye.

Fortunately, I realized their plan was to quickly disqualify me and probably hit the bar for a few beers, so I amped up my energy and focus to answer their tough questions well. One of their key questions was how I managed so many jobs at once while still attending college. They asked how could I have worked three jobs at one time during the summer of 1967. I gave them a complete rundown on who I worked for, what I did, and how many hours I worked every week. That must have piqued their interest because they started to doubt my work experience. They might have thought I was embellishing my work history or "padding my résumé."

For some reason, the interviewers zeroed in on my job at City Auto Stamping, where I worked from May to August of 1967. I told them an abbreviated version of the following story:

After working there for a few weeks, the plant super-intendent, Wally, named me the team leader of the Ford Motor tail assemblies for the rest of the summer. Our shift was the only one consistently turning out good parts because the hydraulic pressure on the press was too low and unable to form them properly without great care. Because so many pieces were needed, we had to work double shifts, seven days a week. It was a grueling and exhausting schedule.

After three months of this, I told my team that I was going to take the weekend off, and the rest of the team decided to follow suit. None of us had been given a day off in months, and we were fatigued to the bone. When I informed our boss, he became visibly upset and had some choice words for me, but he couldn't block us because of our union contract. We all went back to work on Monday, finally a little refreshed.

Early that day, a high-level Ford Motors executive drove into the plant in his beautiful new car. Emerging in his fancy suit and tie, he marched toward me, got right in my face, and barked, "Why the f— can't you make good parts?"

I took a deep breath and said, "I have told management many times that we're constantly losing hydraulic pressure on the press. It goes from three hundred to eighty tons. That isn't enough pressure to make decent parts."

He sized me up and practically spat the words, "You're just a dumb kid, and you don't know what the f— you're talking about!"

I was livid and considered punching him. But somehow I kept my cool, reiterated the problem, and told him I didn't care if he believed it or not. The Ford bigshot stormed off, and my team and I went back to work cranking out the best parts we possibly could.

After telling this story, I suppose the P&G interviewers were convinced of my work experience at City Auto Stamping and the other employment they quizzed me about. And maybe they saw I was not afraid of hard work and not afraid to stand up for myself in tense situations.

> Trust God with your life, your decisions, and your career direction, knowing he will guide you and protect you.

The top guy in the P&G group who interviewed me told me that the company was interested in me, but their quota was filled for new sales employees. He would have to go to the top of the division, the general manager, and the vice president to find me a job.

The P&G guys left, and I didn't hear from anyone for a month and a half. Then, while I was waiting tables at the Boar's Head Bar and drinking beer, the top guy from the P&G team that had interviewed shocked me by showing up and approaching me.

"Hi, I'm Tom from P&G," he said. "Do you remember me from the interview we had five or six weeks ago?"

Extending my hand for a handshake, I answered, "Of course I do. Nice to see you again."

Tom surprised me again by saying, "I've been watching you. Do you always drink this much beer?"

"Actually," I explained, "this is a special occasion. I'm celebrating because I finished my last classes, passed all of my final exams, and will soon receive my BA degree."

Tom smiled and told me P&G was very interested in me. He asked if I was willing to fly to Cincinnati to interview with the top two executives. If they liked me, they would make a job offer at that time.

I had two solid job offers at this point but decided to take the P&G interview before I committed to one of the other offers.

The interview was set for two weeks later. I took my first ever plane flight to Cincinnati and had an hour interview with two key executives—Vice President Bill Coleman along with sales exec Charles Jarvie. They peppered me with questions for an hour, and then the two of them conferred for a minute. Bill said that I should be receiving a job offer in the next few days, concluding by saying, "We're not just offering you a job, but rather a fruitful and productive career."

An offer letter was sent to me on January 5, 1970, and was signed C. L. Jarvie, Manager, Central Division, Central Division Sales Department. My sense was that this was the best company for me to learn the most. In addition, I would work in Chicago, which was quite appealing to me. I accepted the offer and flew to Chicago on January 15, 1970.

A ROUGH START

As head of sales, Mr. Jarvie turned out to be an incredibly demanding man to work for and would demand sky-high sales targets with no room for failure. He was fond of telling his salespeople, "If you fail, you may as well go home dead like a Spartan warrior who had lost a battle."

My new boss, Ray Kimbal, welcomed me to his team by saying, "I've never had anyone work for me whom I hadn't hired. Cole, you'd better be really good or you will be gone in a year."

This was my introduction to the company. And then it got worse.

Kimbal told my manager, Stan Helwig, to give me the worst customers in the Chicago metro area. They gave me 150 customers that mostly were tough as nails, difficult, nasty, and disrespectful. The call book descriptions included Jerk, Rude, A—hole, and so on. Many of my customers were almost impossible to deal with, and in one case I had been told by management to collect money owed. When I tried, one retailer held a weapon in his hand and told me that he would use it if I didn't get out of his store.

> Marry a spouse who will believe in you, love you, and care for you through all the ups and downs of life. You will have a treasure of tremendous value.

My customers included Wieboldt Stores, with the flagship store situated in the worst part of South Chicago. Stan warned me not to make calls later than ten a.m. or I would be at significant risk. I learned how risky the area was on a call that summer when I presented to a product buyer who was a regular customer. He didn't seem his usual self and told me he was feeling distraught because his young son had been killed by a Chicago gang the prior day.

Even some of the customers I sold to in the better parts of Chicago were really tough. One of the shop owners named Irv constantly tried to force me to get P&G to honor coupons that obviously weren't returned by consumers. When I refused to take his invalid coupons, things got nasty.

When I went to call on Irv, he would make me wait a very long time to see him. Finally emerging from his office to see me, he'd look at me and immediately walk away. In my final call with Irv, he called me an obscene name, to which I reciprocated by dishing it back to him. He told me never to call on him or his store again and that he was going to report me to my boss, Stan.

I went back to my apartment and called Stan. "I had an intense confrontation with Irv today," I said. "It got heated, and I called him a bad name."

I explained what happened between Irv and me, and I told him the terrible names we ended up calling each other. Frankly, I expected to be fired for my unprofessional behavior. Stan listened and then started laughing.

"That SOB has had that coming for a long time," Stan said through his laughter. Then he got serious and added, "But, Dave, don't ever do that again."

I'd had enough of the bosses and customers in Chicago. I knew I was going to practically kill myself trying to please the executives—if one of the dangerous customers didn't actually kill me first. Thankfully, just a few weeks after my heated confrontation with Irv, I requested and received a transfer to P&G's Wisconsin district, where I stayed for the next three years.

THE GREATEST BLESSING OF MY MOVE— AND MY LIFE

The most important blessing of the move from Chicago to Milwaukee—by far—was to meet a beautiful young woman named Nancy Gerathy, on October 20, 1970, at a Halloween party. We shared an instant connection, and a first date soon followed. That date was followed by another and another.

Our courtship was thoroughly delightful, filled with meaningful conversations and much laughter, and somehow I convinced this marvelous woman to be my wife. We were married on July 3, 1971, and she has been my loving friend, companion, advisor, and cheerleader for more than fifty years. We have loved one another through all the challenges of a joyful but difficult life. We relocated nine times for nine upward career opportunities. Through all those moves, Nancy was a true partner for me, always believing in me regardless of the risks.

Fast-forward many years. On my last assignment as CEO of Coinstar/Redbox, Nancy and I were both asked to fly to Seattle for the final interview to secure a job offer. Seven years later at my retirement, I went to lunch with a company chairman, and we had a long talk. Near the end, he recommended that I become a speaker in retirement, and he said my opening line should be, "To get a great job, marry a wise and beautiful woman, and turn off the lights."

He admitted he hadn't been totally sure I should be the next CEO during the interview process seven years prior—at least until he met and heard Nancy's answers to his questions. She did as much as I did to land me that job. He was probably more wowed by her than by me.

And his reference to the lights . . . During that final job interview, we were leaving the conference room, and I said, "Shouldn't we turn off the lights?" I suppose he appreciated my frugality.

That chairman's perspective was absolutely spot-on. If asked to give advice to young leaders in the making, my top two gold nuggets of wisdom would be

1. Trust God with your life, your decisions, and your career direction, knowing he will guide you and protect you.

2. Marry a spouse who will believe in you, love you, and care for you through all the ups and downs of life. You will have a treasure of tremendous value.

I am exceedingly grateful that I followed my own advice in both of these ways—though only hindsight has proved how vital each of these decisions has been. And I have been blessed beyond measure by both God and Nancy.

CHANGES AHEAD

In summing up my six years with P&G, they were all extremely challenging years. I worked for demanding, difficult bosses. I worked with difficult, even dangerous customers. But I learned a ton, and God was with me and for me from beginning to end.

I ended up leaving P&G, ready for a change. Procter and Gamble was a solid start because it was considered to be the best company for training sales executives, and I felt like I had earned an MBA from working there. I found, though, there was a hierarchy and rigidity to the company that I didn't enjoy.

Fortunately, a few years with P&G sales became a door opener for a job with another consumer goods company, and I was able find a great next job.

4

A Step Forward

New challenges provide new growth opportunities.

In March of 1976, I joined the Quaker Oats Company as a district manager and was quickly elevated to a senior district manager. A year later, I became area manager for the East Coast. I enjoyed the demands of dealing with food brokers who were the direct contact with our customers, which encompassed virtually every large, medium, or small retailer, including Kroger, A&P, Walmart, Target, and many others.

The team I led worked hard to increase sales of the Quaker product lines. We executed successfully and enjoyed hitting our goals that enabled us to go on the trips the company provided to picturesque places like Italy, Mexico, and Bermuda.

In the fall of 1979, the head of human resources asked if I would fly to Chicago to meet with him. When I got there, he said that he'd never had this situation come up—two divisions of the company had requested that I be promoted to lead their operations. For either job, I would have to live in Chicago.

In one job, I would lead the company's U.S. expansion of the new Quaker Chewy Granola Bar and work directly for a high-level executive. In the second job, I would be responsible for leading the U.S. organization for frozen foods and report to my current boss, who was a manager. It didn't take me long to make the choice. I chose the Chewy Granola Bar option, because I saw it as an opportunity to learn how to run a business.

That proved to be the right choice. I quickly committed to their new business and began to bring in the people who would be on the team. My new boss brought innovative ideas, and I was very interested in growing my ability to manage more than just sales teams. This opportunity was just what I had been hoping for. I would be leading a team that would establish a new product with multiple retailers across the United States and connecting with manufacturing, operations, and marketing departments.

> It is vastly important for leaders to surround themselves with sharp, wise people who bring different perspectives.

For the next seven years, I led the team that provided outstanding execution for the new Chewy Granola Bar rollout. Part of that team included a consultant who was a former president of a division of the Mars Candy Company. This elderly gentleman was outstanding at helping me understand the candy bar and snack market.

The business turned out to be highly successful and a great opportunity to learn and grow. In 1980, though, I got a new boss who demanded that I report to him. Up to that point, I had reported to different bosses I had enjoyed and trusted, and I realized that my new boss was not the right fit for me. For instance, if I asked him a question, he would invariably say, "The answer is obvious." Hearing that response, I never knew if he was patronizing me or if he just didn't know the answer himself. Either way, that standard retort grew increasingly problematic. After several meetings like that, as my confidence in him continued to erode, I realized I couldn't work under this man's leadership, and I decided to move on. Coincidentally (or not), he also moved on the following year.

As I reflect on my time at Quaker, I conclude that it was an excellent place to learn and grow. I appreciated the people I connected with. Two people really stood out. Dennis was a great salesperson I hired who had an amazing ability to reach very high-level executives. With his skills, we were able to grow the Walmart business five times larger than it had been previously. I called him a Seal Team guy. He was so good that I hired him at my next job at Weyerhaeuser/Paragon.

Another brilliant team member was Dan, a young man who possessed a keen understanding of future markets. I remember the day he told me water would be a huge market soon.

"Believe me, Dave," he insisted, "bottled water is going to be the next big thing in the beverage market. It can be produced and marketed in many variations—carbonated, flavored, infused with vitamins."

My response: "But water is free, so why would anyone pay for it?"

He explained all of his rationales, and time has shown how right he was and what an acute prognosticator he was. And it reinforced to me the vast importance for leaders to surround themselves with sharp, wise people who bring different perspectives.

My team had done an outstanding job and had secured great distribution and relationships in all classes of trade, including grocery, drug, convenience, and mass retailers.

Anywhere candy bars were sold, Quaker Chewy Granola Bars were in distribution.

TIME TO MOVE ON

After a brief stop working with a consulting firm, I was contacted by headhunter James Meade in the summer of 1985. Jim asked if I'd be interested in becoming head of retail sales with the Peter Paul Cadbury company, manufacturer of numerous chocolate confections and other food products. I was eager to pursue the opportunity because I would be back in a leadership role.

At first, though, Cadbury concerned me because the company had a less-than-stellar reputation in the trade and had lacked good management in its prior administration. At that time, Cadbury was the third largest chocolate provider in the United States with about 19 percent of the market. The company was owned by the Cadbury family with Sir Adrian Cadbury serving as CEO.

I felt better about its reputation when Jim Meade shared with me that the whole company was now staffed with outstanding people led by a seasoned and exceptional leader, William I. Savel.

Jim Meade had done an incredibly thorough search and asked sixty organizations in the candy business who would be the best sales leader. My name came up about fifty times because of my team's outstanding execution on the Quaker Chewy Granola Bar. Because sales was the weakest function at Cadbury, they were looking for a strong leader to improve it.

Bill Savel was named president of Cadbury USA on March 21, 1986, and quickly assembled a top-level management team that turned out to be the best team I had ever worked with. In my time there, we not only worked together but also had fun and celebrated each other.

Bill brought considerable experience and success in turning around underachieving companies. Bill and I met in his office and had an extensive conversation regarding the challenges of the turnaround and of his philosophy of leadership.

I admit that I felt intimidated by Bill and his credentials. He was a man of great honesty, candor, brilliance, humility, command of every situation, and sense of humor. I walked out of his office wanting to work for him, knowing I would learn so much from him. He never disappointed me. More than any other job, I learned from him about how to run a company, create strong relationships with colleagues, and keep top executive teams aligned to execute the team's plan effectively and efficiently.

Under Bill's leadership, Cadbury experienced a remarkable turnaround. Market share improved, new products were rolled out, revenue increased significantly, and staff morale rebounded. It was one of those rare situations in corporate life where nearly every employee, top to bottom, felt excited about coming to work and believed in the future of the company.

But beyond the success of Cadbury, great sadness came in August of 1988. Adrian Cadbury decided to sell the company to the Hershey Chocolate Company, which was vying to be the largest seller of chocolate products in the United States. The acquisition of Cadbury made Hershey 20 percent larger than their closest competitor, M&M Mars. Hershey went all in with their expansion ambitions, since the cost of the Cadbury acquisition was four times the valuation of the company. It was as if someone bought your house and gave you four times market value.

It was a terrific deal for Sir Adrian and the Cadbury family, but our entire team felt extremely disappointed. We had come together with the superb leadership of Bill Savel and worked incredibly hard to improve the company in every aspect, including product, quality, packaging, and advertising, and to vastly improve relationships with all our retail partners. But we knew we wouldn't be able to continue on as a team. As with most corporate mergers and acquisitions, there were departmental reorganizations, employee layoffs, revamping of procedures, and new leaders brought in.

> It was one of those rare situations in corporate life where nearly every employee, top to bottom, felt excited about coming to work and believed in the future of the company.

I felt blessed to be one of the few people on the team able to stay connected to Bill. Hershey had asked me to stay on with the company, but Bill told me they probably wouldn't give me the job I wanted, which was vice president of sales. Because I trusted Bill's judgment, I finished my work and left Hershey in January of 1989.

Though I was greatly disappointed to no longer be on Bill's team, God had another plan for me, and I almost blew it. As usual, God gave me grace and provided me with two chances at an opportunity.

5

Exhausted, Then Energized

Amid tough transitions, God brings renewal.

In early December 1986, while wrapping up my work at Cadbury, I was asked to meet a headhunter who wanted to interview me as a candidate to lead the Weyerhaeuser baby diaper sales team. He asked me to meet him at Los Angeles International Airport (LAX), and I agreed.

Prior to the interview, I'd conducted many meetings with dozens of Cadbury salespeople regarding the company's sale to Hershey. It had been a full week of discussing tense issues and the coming changes for the sales crew. By the time I finished the week, I felt exhausted and drained.

Then I showed up to at the airport to meet with the headhunter. We discussed the opportunity and challenges with the Weyerhaeuser position for two hours. Being so tired, I wasn't on my game and didn't make a great impression on him. As a result, I didn't hear anything from him when I returned home to Connecticut.

A few weeks later, Jim Meade, my former headhunter, called to asked me if I would fly to Seattle to meet the key Weyerhaeuser team.

"Thanks, Jim," I said, "but I'm pretty sure they don't want me, because they never called me back. No communication at all."

"Actually," he replied, "the guy you interviewed with could tell you are very knowledgeable about the market landscape and the challenges within the division. But he didn't think you had 'a tiger in your tank,' as he put."

I felt taken aback for a moment, and then said, "I've never been accused of not having 'a tiger in my tank,' but I have to admit my tiger wasn't very fierce that day. I was totally spent."

I told Jim I was pursuing two other opportunities, and Nancy and I were not interested in moving to Seattle, which was Weyerhaeuser's home. But being the competitive person that I am, I now wanted to win that job offer and prove my passion, energy, and drive.

"Set up the next meeting," I told Jim, "and I'll make sure my tiger is ready to pounce."

I spent the next four days studying up on the company, market, challenges, and opportunities. I flew to Seattle on Sunday and arrived at the offices Monday morning ready to go. I met with the team, comprised of five top executives. The interview was scheduled for three hours, and there were a hundred questions I would be expected to answer. I don't remember the first question, but I do remember that I spent forty-five minutes answering it. They said I gave a thorough answer to the first question and had probably answered many of their others already, but I continued to answer all the questions they wanted to throw at me.

At the end, I thanked them for their time and went to call Jim Meade as he requested. He said I had done very well and they wanted me back the next week for an interview with Bobby Abraham, the president of the division, for a job offer.

The afternoon I arrived, the Pacific Northwest had never looked better. As I drove down the freeway, I felt overjoyed taking in the glimmering snow on Mount Rainier and the Olympic Mountains, plus the beauty of the Puget Sound. I arrived on time and spent a couple of hours with Bobby Abraham, who reported directly to George Weyerhaeuser, president of the entire company.

As both of us are men of faith, Bobby and I connected well during the interview. He had come to the Northwest a number of years prior, bringing many innovative ideas to make the baby diaper division a huge part of Weyerhaeuser. The diaper business had a plan to use Japanese technology to launch a superior product. The division was building a highly capable team to compete with Procter and Gamble, the world market leader, and Kimberly Clark, second in the market. It was an audacious vision, and I found myself excited about the project.

I received an excellent offer, which I accepted. My ever-supportive wife and I prepared for another cross-country move for another exciting opportunity.

EXPANDING ROLES

Bobby and I worked together for ten years and had great respect for one another. My first year, he seemed impressed with my ability to work well beyond the sales division. As a result, he gave me responsibilities beyond my job that included marketing, manufacturing, and purchasing. In fact, after the first year, he asked me if I would run operations. He gave me a week to think about it, and I came back with a plan for improvements. He agreed and the organization became far more effective by doing less but doing it very well.

I felt very pleased when I received the Weyerhaeuser Company Leadership Award for demonstrating values through actions. A year later, I was recognized for my unique contributions to the company.

In 1996 Weyerhaeuser made the decision to refocus the company to just wood products, prompting many subsidiary companies to be closed. Since the baby division was quite profitable, it was not shut down and, in fact, would be spun off in an IPO. This meant that it would be a separate company and stock would be sold to the public.

I was named president and chief operating officer by the board of directors, and Bobby, our CFO, and I took the Weyerhaeuser baby diaper business through an IPO. This was an exciting time and a great opportunity for Bobby and me to become significant owners. The IPO enabled us to sell shares in the new company, named Paragon Trade Brands, and we sold shares to people throughout the world.

> In the rough-and-tumble world of retail sales, where millions of dollars are on the line each year, a company's circumstances can go from lofty to lousy with the snap of a finger.

We had made strong inroads in the Sam's Club baby diaper business, which boosted revenue, but we had little of the Walmart business. As I pondered the conundrum, the name Dennis came to mind. We had worked together at Quaker Oats, and I had heard that he had been promoted to a higher-level sales executive position. He and his team did great work on the Chewy Granola Bar campaign and getting that product to market.

Reaching out to Dennis, I learned to my surprise that he had been asked to leave Quaker over a disagreement with top management about where to place Gatorade in stores. Dennis insisted that the product should be placed in a particular location, and the execs dug in on another location. The dispute ended with Dennis's departure.

Quaker's loss was my gain. I asked Dennis if he would like to work with me, explaining that we had a great opportunity with Walmart, but we needed a pro like him to lead the venture. He was quite excited and said he wanted the job. I made it clear to him and the company that Dennis would report directly to me, the COO.

AN UNUSUAL APPROACH

Typical of Dennis, he joined our team with a highly unusual plan in mind. He went to his local Walmart and asked the manager if he could work for free in the store for the next couple of months to learn the Walmart systems from the ground up. He explained that he served as a sales executive with Paragon and would be approaching Walmart buyers in Bentonville, Arkansas. The store manager loved the idea and asked the execs in Bentonville if that would be allowed. Impressed, the second highest executive in the U.S. Walmart stores division said he wanted to meet Dennis for coffee any time he was in town. With that solid connection for Dennis, he introduced me to several key players over the next few years.

Initially, a number of companies had Walmart's private label baby diaper business, but eventually we got all of it, along with strong relationships with all of the key executives. Walmart became our largest customer, and Dennis was a hero both at Walmart and at Paragon.

I anticipated excellent business with Walmart, and it turned out to exceed my expectations. Dennis truly understood the business, often educating me about infant diapers, toddler diapers, hypoallergenic diapers, training pants, and countless other variations. Based on his conversations with retail buyers and customers, I would go to key people in our company and demand we bring new products quickly to the market. This was a very important aspect of the product lines in Walmart and with other customers.

DISASTER STRIKES

Though business grew and profits soared, the competition was vicious. We battled P&G and Kimberly Clark for market share for many years, gaining more and more respect and revenue. Those years stand out as some of the most successful and enjoyable of my working life.

Unfortunately, in the rough-and-tumble world of retail sales, where millions of dollars are on the line each year, a company's circumstances can go from lofty to lousy with the snap of a finger. This proved to be true for me and our entire Paragon team.

In the mid-1990s, Paragon became embroiled in a legal fight with P&G and Kimberly Clark in a patent infringement suit. The suit centered on diaper design features that ensured the diapers would not leak. Litigation by the plaintiffs claimed improper use—or theft—of specific aspects by the defendant (Paragon), with many legal discourses involving elastic threads, zigzag stitching, and absorbent materials. The suit slithered its way through the system with numerous delays and reams of arcane legal briefs only patent attorneys could fathom.

If average consumers had learned about this lawsuit, they would have yawned and shrugged. But executives and employees who might be directly impacted by such a lawsuit felt fearful shivers coursing down their spine and a churning gut keeping them awake each night.

Our lawyers had assured the executive team that we had an excellent case and encouraged us not to worry. But that assurance proved hollow and misguided. On the last day of December in 1998, as I was working at my desk, I received a call from Bobby, the CEO. The message was the worst news I could have imagined.

"Dave," he said, sounding completely deflated, "I'm sorry to be the one to tell you this, but P&G won the lawsuit against Paragon. We both know what this means."

> Executives and employees who might be directly impacted by such a lawsuit felt fearful shivers coursing down their spine and a churning gut keeping them awake each night.

The results were disastrous for the company—and for the thousand or more employees who had put money into our stock, which was suddenly no longer worth anything.

I had become a millionaire prior to this based on the company stock, and after years of legal wrangling and one verdict from a judge, I lost 95 percent of my net worth. Adding salt to an open wound, the company's legal team would need to investigate the possibility that we would lose our houses. This was definitely one of the worst days of our lives.

I felt shaken to my core and deeply concerned with all the losses for our creditors, investors, customers, and employees—and whether the company could even be saved. After a painful meeting with our key executives, it was clear that the company could be saved but would have to reorganize under Chapter 11 bankruptcy protocols.

This changed many aspects of my life. I resigned my position as Paragon president and chief operating officer to become a board member of the new Paragon that emerged from Chapter 11. I was a member of the board that had to let go of Bobby Abraham when the company was acquired by the private equity firm Wellspring Capital Management. It was an extremely challenging job and time in my life.

The silver lining—though hard to see any at the time—was that the company survived and those who invested in its stock would keep our homes. (I will share more in chapter 22 about how I survived and grew through that devastating time.)

During the time that Paragon was going through the disastrous Chapter 11 process, Bill Savel, my former boss at Cadbury, called me to ask how I was doing. Bill had been on the board of Paragon for a few years when the company went public and had gotten to know Bobby.

Through the years, Bill had become a trusted ally and a close friend of mine. I told Bill I was not doing well at all, but I would like to collect my bonus of $1 million that required me to stay with the company through the reorganization to Chapter 11, which would likely be a two-year period. It would be a chance to dig out of the financial hole I had shockingly fallen into. It had been an excruciating experience for me, and my heart and God's Spirit told me it was time to move on.

"Dave, you're an exceptional leader with much more to bring to another company—and the world," he told me. "You can do better than stay at Paragon through the bankruptcy recovery. You deserve more than Paragon is offering, even though that bonus is a nice carrot dangling out there for you."

I shared with Bill my chief concern and biggest heartache. "I don't want to abandon the team that I assembled and the hundreds of people who have trusted me to lead this company—and trust me to lead them back to a place of stability and prosperity."

"You more than anymore led this company to a place of stability and prosperity in the first place," he replied. "If you choose to leave, you're not abandoning anyone. Let go of any false guilt you might have, and free yourself to do whatever you feel is right and best."

Upon reflection, I realized Bill was right. The words of my wise friend and advisor confirmed what my heart and God's voice were telling me. It was time to move on to the next assignment and adventure.

6

Redirected Once Again

After financial disaster, another door opens.

B ased on my conversation with Bill, I reconnected with Jim Meade, the superb headhunter who had assisted me so well in previous transitions. Over dinner, Jim discussed an opportunity at Torbitt and Castleman, a midsize manufacturer of private label goods, producing syrups, Mexican sauces, jams and jellies, barbecue sauces, and similar food products for Walmart, Kroger, and other large retailers. The owners of the company were called The Northern Group, located in Seattle.

Jim indicated they were looking for an individual with skills like mine to become the president of two companies, one located in Kentucky and the other in Wisconsin. Jim recommended I take a meeting with one of the owners and the president of the company. The current president was set to become CEO of all of the Northern Group food companies, including a food manufacturing company in Grand Rapids, Michigan.

In late August of 1999, I jumped on a plane from Atlanta to Louisville after learning how to pronounce "Looavul" (definitely not "Louieville") and met with the key leaders and team members. I felt this could be a good fit. I was impressed with the operating folks, the sales group, and especially the HR director. Subsequently, I was offered an excellent financial package and decided to take the job and move to Louisville.

After my grueling experience with Paragon, I needed to assume a much less demanding leadership role. My time at Torbitt and Castleman ended up being just what the doctor ordered. The company was much less complicated, with just two operating businesses and five hundred people in two plants. In addition, the key executive team was well staffed, the HR team excelled in personnel development, and quality control was excellent. Bill, the CEO of the organization, was effective but had too much on his plate.

> I jumped on a plane from Atlanta to Louisville after learning how to pronounce "Looavul."

REALITY CHECK

On my second day as president of Torbitt, I led the key executive staff meeting. I asked the assembled dozen leaders how we were going to deliver the dollar profit goal the owner of the company told me was critical to meet.

Silence ensued, and the people looked awkwardly around at each other. Finally, someone spoke up.

"That goal is simply not doable," the person said, "and we all told the CEO as much in our last meeting with him."

Someone else chimed in, "Realistically, we can achieve only 20 percent of the revenue goal he set."

Obviously, it came as a surprise that the CEO and the leadership team were so far apart on the revenue goal. That evening, I spent a lot of time thinking amount how to deal with the difference between the CEO's expectations and the team's number. I decided to call the CEO the next day and let him know of the significant difference between the two projections.

After talking to him, he asked the head of sales, Brett, and me to fly to Seattle where his office was located. We arrived in Seattle and spent the next three days and nights working through a realistic plan to hit the required number. The plan included increasing revenue and reducing costs. We took the plan back to the management team, explaining how we could make it happen. One significant part of the plan was to increase our business with key customers, especially Walmart and Kroger.

BACK TO BENTONVILLE WE GO

I had traveled to Walmart headquarters in Bentonville, Arkansas, many times over the years, so I knew the lay of the land. I also knew how extremely important these meetings were, with relationships needing to be developed and high-stakes decisions on the line. This time, Brett and I had to convince the Walmart executive responsible for buying Walmart private-label food products that we could provide the excellent goods and services required by them.

Before arriving, Brett told me, "I've met with this executive before, and he's a tough one. He's harder to crack than a bank vault. No-nonsense, no BS, no punches pulled."

"Thanks for the heads-up," I responded. "I know the type. I've been in sales for nineteen years and have dealt with many impossible-to-please buyers. We'll win him over."

The executive turned out to be exactly as Brett had warned—tough as nails.

The meeting was planned for an hour, and the man spent two hours and fifty-seven minutes telling us in excruciating detail why our company was a lousy supplier. He concluded by saying, "Sorry, gentlemen, you just don't have much chance of getting more Walmart business based on your current performance."

He then looked at his watch and said, "Now it's your turn. You have three minutes."

I spent the next three minutes assuring him as persuasively as I could that we would deliver quality products and services on time and with utmost excellence.

> It came as a surprise that the CEO and the leadership team were so far apart on the revenue goal.

He then upped the ante. "If you don't achieve outstanding results within the next six months, you'll lose our business. Period."

I met with this Walmart executive six months into our "probationary" period, and he told me we had satisfied Walmart with our results and directed me to just keep doing what we were doing. We increased the Walmart business substantially during the year I was president.

SHORT BUT SWEET

I ended up spending only a little more than a year with Torbitt and Castleman. The initial business plan that the owner presented to me when I was interviewing for the job included the purchase of a much larger company to add to the existing family of companies. He thought the acquisition was a sure thing, but in the end it went to the largest player in the market. I had learned that Torbitt's CEO often had lofty plans that didn't pan out.

Without the addition of that company, Torbitt was too small to compete in the marketplace of the future, so I recommended that they sell it. It was sold to the same large company that had purchased the one Torbitt lost out on. While I was asked to stay and lead the combined operations in Louisville, it became clear to me that I would not be a good fit with the new leadership. Therefore, I got my release and pay from the Northern Group.

For the first time in many years, I had a summer off. I played golf, spent time with our Louisville friends, and took a wonderful vacation with Nancy.

Alas, with my summer vacation drawing to a close, I developed a résumé and sent out seven hundred letters to various companies. I received about fifteen responses, with only two opportunities that interested me. I also tried to find work in Louisville, where Nancy and I hoped to stay with our new group of friends. After connecting with lots of people and not finding anything suitable, I realized I would have to expand my job search.

7

Finishing Strong

*The final chapter in a career is sometimes
the most fulfilling.*

In late June 2001, I sat watching the U.S. Open golf tournament when I received a call from an executive of one of the best search companies in the world. He asked me to meet him in Washington, D.C., as he was working to fill President George W. Bush's cabinet and administration.

I hasten to add that, no, he was definitely not considering me for a role in the Bush administration! He wanted to discuss with me a job opening in the Seattle area.

We met a couple of days later and spent two hours discussing my background, skills, and experience, discovering we had much in common. We were both born in 1947 in Toledo, Ohio. I was born on the west side; he was born on the north side. We both graduated from Miami of Ohio University in 1969, and we both went to work for Procter and Gamble as our first job out of college.

As our meeting ended, he said I was a perfect fit for the CEO position at Coinstar, the company that manufactures and distributes machines that help consumers convert loose change into paper currency or gift cards. But, he said, it would take until early fall for the job to open up. He asked me to hang on and call him if I had any questions or concerns. Turns out, I had no other job offers except the role of president of Daisy Air Rifle Company located in Arkansas, which didn't sound like a good fit.

The Coinstar position did open up in late summer, and early in the morning on September 11, 2001, Nancy and I boarded a plane scheduled to fly from Louisville to Seattle. The plane, however, never left the airport because of the terrorist attacks that day. We went home and watched the horror unfold on television. With no plans and no ability to travel, we were glued to the TV for a week.

Immediately after air travel resumed, Nancy and I became some of the only flyers. It felt eerie to be in Chicago's usually bustling O'Hare Airport with few stores open and only a handful of people there.

Once we arrived in Seattle, I had interviews with the board chair and senior staff, and Nancy was interviewed by the board chair. Later, the board chair called to offer me the CEO position, which I accepted. Nancy and I began preparing for yet another relocation.

EARLY CHALLENGES

Coinstar was quite a challenge from October 2001 to August 2002. The company had been a start-up in 1991 and included a number of unusual practices, to say the least.

The company had been led by strong young leaders who were very sure of themselves and the unique service they provided to retailers and consumers. In addition, they believed their service was impossible to duplicate by competition. The top leaders, especially the young man whose idea it was to provide consumers self-service coin counting and make a lot of money in the process, believed the company would never have competition due to the many patents held by Coinstar.

The company had lost almost all of their key people, and I learned much later that there were problems with nearly all of high-level management. Beginning early on my first day on the job, several irate investors called me directly to express their anger over a contentious situation, often with vehement words and a harsh tone of voice. It turned out that the prior CEO had not told investors that the company had developed another product it was pouring substantial funds into without the investors' knowledge.

> It became abundantly clear to me that I needed to institute changes not only to the business practices but also to the corporate culture.

Being brand-new to the company and not understanding all the dynamics, the best I could do was listen patiently, offer reassurance, and try to begin to establish better relationships. I learned the organization had been through a difficult time with certain primary investors who had fired the key officers and most of the board of directors.

The board chair let me know that he and the rest of the current board would be leaving soon and replaced by new board members chosen by activist investors from the Seattle area and Wall Street.

Unfortunately, I was not experienced in dealing with this type of board. It was comprised of all local people, including two who were part of the interview team that hired me. I felt that the hiring team would be supportive, but those I had not met were of some concern. Despite this, I believed I could win them over with my years of experience and strength in leading people.

In addition to my concerns about the board, I quickly became alarmed by several of the company practices. For one, employees celebrated every Friday afternoon with alcoholic drinks provided by the company. The partying began midafternoon and continued until quitting time. Common sense would raise many red flags with this weekly tradition, starting with lost productivity and ending with the dangers of inebriated employees driving home at the end of the workday.

Needless to say, I had significant concerns about this boozy ritual, regardless if the prior CEO encouraged it. I called the board chair, who had no idea this was happening and agreed with me that it needed to stop ASAP. I put a stop to the Friday frolicking despite the risk of being regarding as the new Chief Executive Killjoy.

In spite of some odd protocols, the company was doing quite well in a unique business space. The loose change conversion machines produced big profits for the company. Deducting a percentage from each transaction, the machines in total processed around $3 billion worth of coins annually. With a transaction fee of 12 percent or more, that equates to hefty corporate revenues each year.

DEEPENING CONCERNS

Coinstar's founder had innovative ideas, but I had apprehensions as to how the system worked in the field. So I sought information by taking the head of operations out for coffee to talk.

After getting a general overview, I asked him, "How do you evaluate employees?"

"Our field people are evaluated on how well their machines are working," he answered. "They have to be at the locations on a regular basis to check the machines and to know if the store manager is pleased with their work."

That methodology seemed vague to me, but I moved on for now.

"Tell me about how you measure cost," I said. "How do you track cost for maintaining the machines, repairing malfunctioning machines, compensating repair technicians, and so forth?"

He looked puzzled and said, "Well, we don't measure cost."

I was floored and told him it's standard business practice to manage cost.

On the way back to the office, I asked him to develop a cost study and bring it to me as soon as possible. I explained clearly what information I wanted to see. I added that I'd like for him to develop a better relationship with his boss, as the cost management issue seemed to be an ongoing problem.

After more than a month, I hadn't received any response to my request. I asked my administrative assistant if the head of operations had delivered any kind of report, and the answer was no. The next day, I met with the head of operations and asked why he hadn't responded to me.

"Oh, sorry," he said. "I've been too busy."

"It's been a whole month since I asked you to create a report, giving you clear direction for what I was looking for," I told him. "If you were too busy to respond to me after a month, you need to be working someplace else."

Then I told him I needed to terminate his employment with the company.

Another example of the hubris and nonchalant attitude I encountered came from the head of sales. I asked him how the sales team was doing in getting the Coinstar machines into Walmart.

"We don't want to be in Walmart," he replied. "We approached Walmart a while back, but we didn't get anywhere. It wasn't worth the time to pursue it anymore, and we decided we don't need them."

Again I was floored. *Not worth the time? We don't need Walmart?* Unbelievable.

I explained that Walmart is the biggest retailer in the world and we did indeed need them to expand our business. He still didn't see the point in going after Walmart business, but I made it abundantly clear that we would be doing everything in our power to get into their stores.

It became abundantly clear to me that I needed to institute changes not only to the business practices but also to the corporate culture. We needed to move from highly relaxed to highly focused.

ANOTHER PAINFUL LEARNING EXPERIENCE

In the fall of 2002, the chairman of the board informed me that the board was considering firing me and replacing me with a new CEO. The chair asked me to have lunch at the Seattle Tennis Club, and after we finished lunch, he revealed the board member who had opened the discussion of replacing me. He and his boss, who owned 10 percent of the Coinstar shares, felt I was not making the progress they had expected. The instigating board member also had convinced another member to vote with him.

This came as a gut punch to me. I asked the chair what were the specific issues that concerned the board members. The chair told me there were two reasons. The first was that I was not making the progress they had expected, and the second was that I had told this specific board member to stop telling the employee in charge of product development what new products he should bring forward. I'd had a conversation with this board member previously to remind him that this was not his role as a board member.

> I told him, "You may kill me in the course of getting me fired, but I will take off your arm and leg in the process."

I always had the feeling that he wanted my job. He would typically spend too much time in the organization talking with people extensively and in some cases interfering with the productivity we needed to deliver as a company.

"I can tell you I will not resign my position," I told the board chairman. "If the board wants me gone, it will have to fire me and provide me with my full severance."

The man didn't respond, so I added, "If I am let go and asked by a search firm or key retailers about the company, I'll tell the unvarnished truth as I see it. I'll explain that the company needs significant improvement and the board is a big problem because of certain key shareholders."

With the discussion finished, I returned to the office and got on the phone. I called each of the directors and repeated what I had told the chair. These phone calls were very difficult, but I told each of them that I would not resign my position. If fired, I would not provide any kind of help to the new CEO. Most important, I said I also believed I had the ability to make the company far more effective, efficient, and profitable.

I had an extra message to the director who was responsible for the insurrection. I told him, "You may kill me in the course of getting me fired, but I will take off your arm and leg in the process."

After those few minutes on the phone with him, I didn't talk to him for the next five years. Subsequently, the board met without me some thirty times to determine my future. Even though I was a board member, I was not allowed to attend meetings or vote on my fate. I decided to ignore everything except continuing to improve relationships with the shareholders and customers and to improve the company's effectiveness as much as possible.

After months of vacillation and deliberation, the board decided on February 1 of 2003 to give me a new contract.

UPSIDES AMID DOWNSIDES

Some positives emerged from all of this pain and turmoil. My prayers became more frequent and fervent, and the more I connected with God, the better I felt. It's often said that we grow most, spiritually and emotionally, through hardship, and that was true for me during that painful time. I leaned on God for guidance, wisdom, and patience. I listened for God's voice and looked for his leading. My spiritual life deepened and expanded in ways it never had before.

Practically speaking, my mind continually focused on ways to be a better leader and help the company reach its potential. I came to realize that we needed to have more products and services in order to be significant to Walmart and other mass merchandisers. In addition, the company needed to expand into other countries—Western Europe and Canada, at a minimum. In order to achieve this, we would have to bring on talented people capable of opening doors in those parts of the world.

All of these dreams and plans came to fruition. We expanded into other countries including Canada, the UK, and France. We brought in more talented people and looked at many other businesses to acquire. Our people researched businesses involving shredder machines, special shopping carts for kids, money transfer businesses, key duplicators, and many others.

Though we bought a number of companies, in the end there were two worth noting—a big loser and a big winner. The loser was the acquisition of a company that owned the claw-grabber machines seen at the front of large stores and some arcades. You drop coins in the slot and try to grab a small stuffed animal, ball, or other toy with the mechanical claw. This proved to be a poor investment because the margins were very low and the machines tended to malfunction frequently. I took a lot of flack from the board for this lousy investment.

The big winner was the acquisition of Redbox, the dispenser of DVD movies found in front of grocery stores, convenience stores, fast-food restaurants, and other high-traffic locations. At the time, Redbox was mostly owned by the McDonald's Corporation, with shared ownership from other entities. The CEO of Redbox came to Coinstar to ask for help in expanding their U.S. distribution. We agreed on the condition that we would have the right to purchase the rest of Redbox if McDonald's decided to sell it.

McDonald's had an outstanding product in Redbox, and Coinstar had relationships or deep connections with many large retailers. We became strong partners with the Redbox team and over the years helped McDonald's place the machines in virtually every significant U.S. retailer.

Fortuitously for Coinstar, when large shareholders of McDonald's demanded that the company sell off Redbox, we gladly purchased it. We were aware that other technologies would eventually replace DVDs and there would probably be ten to fifteen years of life for the product. But for many years (until DVDs went the way of cassette tapes and CDs), those red vending machines were ubiquitous across America and raked in many billions of dollars.

Our investors were extremely pleased, but more importantly, millions of our customers loved the Redbox product and value.

HEARING GOD'S VOICE OF REASSURANCE

It hadn't been a smooth and easy ride to achieve the eventual Redbox success. We had spent lots of time and energy making large shareholders of the stock believe that the Coinstar company was in a strong place and that we would provide strong earnings with a Redbox acquisition. In December, though, as I was watching TV with Nancy, my mind focused on business and I felt deeply concerned. We had put in tremendous effort with Walmart and had convinced them to install both Redbox and Coinstar machines in all their superstores throughout the U.S.

However, I had just been in Bentonville to meet with the new top U.S. executive, who told me in no uncertain terms that he would not put Coinstar or Redbox machines in any of their stores because he was committed to "cleaning" the U.S. stores. He wanted to reduce clutter in the stores, consolidate operations and options, and streamline the customer experience.

It had been a terrible meeting. Even after I tried three times to get him to change his mind, he simply would not.

So as I watched TV that night, I was focused on work problems. I started saying a silent prayer. I don't think I said anything about Walmart in my prayer, but I asked for God's guidance and direction. I expressed my anxieties and asked God to ease my burden. I must have said my short little prayer a few hundred times before I finally heard a response. Words were spoken into my right ear: *"Dave, I'm here, and I'm with you."*

Astounded, I stopped praying and started thinking that this must have been the voice of God. I had never heard it before, but I was sure it was God. I never doubted that the words came from God and were for me: *"I'm here, and I'm with you."* I knew that I could cast my anxieties on him, and he would help me make wise decisions if I sought his help.

About six weeks later in February, the Walmart executive who had been so adamant about not putting Coinstar and Redbox machines in the stores reversed his decision. We signed a large number of contracts to have them installed. Soon, Walmart began placing thousands of our coin and movie machines in stores across the United States.

Wall Street went crazy with the good news. At that time, most of the Wall Street traders were encouraging their clients to sell us short. After this happened, our stock went up tremendously. It was the most amazing turnaround that had ever happened on my watch in the business.

We had quarterly meetings with all Coinstar employees where I gave them a review of the business. This particular quarter they were very happy to hear the news of our stock shooting up because of the inroads with Walmart.

"DAVE, IT'S TIME"

After several years of successful and enjoyable leadership, I made a decision to retire after a bitter proxy fight, where one faction of shareholders sought to gain control of the organization. While management believed we would win the proxy fight based on the intelligence we had gleaned from key investors, we decided we should award one seat on the board of directors to our adversaries.

We decided to accept onto the board the one person we considered to be fair and reasonable among the opposing faction. We had hoped doing so would facilitate better terms with the investor who held a significant percent of our shares.

The annual meeting with the board and shareholders was held in 2008, and the single new member of the board was there and responding quite reasonably. I shared my thoughts with him, noting that he was now part of the team and we were no longer adversaries. Our goal was to be constructive and work together with the rest of the board and increase the value of the company.

I left that annual meeting and headed back to my office. I sat down for a few minutes, feeling exhausted and spent. I rubbed my extremely painful shoulder, injured during a volleyball game at our executive retreat. For weeks, I had been seeing a doctor and physical therapist to get some relief from the pain.

I leaned over my desk, put my head down, and again heard the voice of God. This time he said, "Dave, it's time." I knew what this meant.

I decided at that moment to talk with Nancy as soon as I got home. If she felt like I did, I would quickly meet with the board chair and resign my position. Nancy was in agreement with me. I'd developed enough experience—enough spiritual listening skills—to know it was God's will.

Early the next morning, I sat down with Paul Davis, who had been hired as my replacement for my eventual retirement in two years. Paul had been working with me for a year to learn the business. I shared with him my decision to resign. Paul had extensive experience in public companies and assured me he was comfortable taking over my job at that point.

Later that week, Paul and I went to the Seattle condo of the chairman of the board, Keith, to talk through the issue. He expressed concern and didn't want me to leave, but he understood and felt it was the right thing to do. Keith said he first wanted to connect with the rest of the board and get their take on the timing and when to go public with the announcement.

The plan was to release the information to the public in December. The day I planned to announce my decision turned out to be the day that Lehman Brothers collapsed, the market crashed, and so did the value of most stocks. Because of the volatility of the market, and fear among shareholders and the public, I was asked to stay with the company for a while to ensure things stayed stable.

In fact, because of the volatile market, the Coinstar board did not want to take the risk of buying the rest of the shares from McDonald's. However, after numerous board meetings, we decided to acquire the rest of the company shares, with Coinstar becoming the sole owner of Redbox.

I ended up leaving the company on March 30, 2009, pleased and relieved to turn responsibility over to Paul. He is an incredibly gifted executive who did all the right things to grow the company, which included integrating the Coinstar and Redbox divisions. Paul and I remain friends to this day.

MOVING ON TO NEW ADVENTURES

After my departure from Coinstar, I wondered for a while if I should pursue another role in corporate leadership. I wondered if I was ready to hang it up. Although I had grown weary of many battles with boards, endless mind-numbing meetings, and numerous relocations, I still felt I had "a tiger in my tank"—energy and passion to step into a new position and lead with confidence.

But then I reflected on God's clear words to me: "Dave, it's time." At the moment I heard those words, I thought God was telling me it was time to move on from Coinstar. I came to realize, though, he was telling me, "Dave, it's time to open up a new chapter in your life. It's time to shift your focus and pursue new adventures. It's time to use your leadership skills in different ways."

In the epilogue of this book, I will share how "retirement" became one of the most fulfilling seasons of my life. For now, I want to emphasize that retirement is often seen as the end of a long and fulfilling career, but it's also the beginning of a new chapter filled with exciting possibilities. Rather than slowing down, retirement offers the chance to explore new adventures and open doors that may have been previously out of reach due to work commitments. This stage of life is an opportunity to pursue passions, discover new interests, and embrace the freedom to serve in ways previously unavailable.

All of this was true for me and can be for everyone. There is no need to ever stop learning, growing, and serving.

Part Two

Lessons Learned, Wisdom Won

8

Love the People You Lead

Transformative leadership begins by truly caring about your team members.

Years ago, fairly early in my career, I found myself at the helm of a rapidly growing company. The corporate culture was fast-paced, hard-charging, with high expectations for all staff members.

Not surprisingly, my days were packed with attending back-to-back meetings, analyzing spreadsheets, and ensuring that we hit our sales goals and financial targets. I prided myself on my efficiency and ability to drive results. My focus was sharp, and my determination to see the company succeed was unwavering. I believed that if I kept my head down and pushed forward, everything else would fall into place.

But as I raced through the daily grind, something was missing. The energy in the office was tense. People seemed disengaged, and turnover was higher than I wanted to admit. I dismissed it as a byproduct of the fast-paced environment we were in. My interactions with my team were strictly professional—I kept conversations focused on tasks and deadlines, rarely asking about their lives or well-being. After all, we were here to work, not to socialize.

Then, one morning, I received news that one of my key managers, Sarah, had been hospitalized. She had been with the company for decades and was one of the hard-est-working people on the team. I realized I didn't even know what had happened to her. I was too caught up in meetings and numbers to notice that she had been under immense stress. Her absence was sudden, and it hit me harder than I expected.

Out of a sense of obligation more than anything else, I decided to visit her in the hospital. When I arrived, I was struck by how frail she looked. She was lying in bed, surrounded by flowers and cards from her colleagues, people who clearly cared about her much more than I had allowed myself to. Sarah seemed surprised to see me and greeted me enthusiastically. After we exchanged pleasantries, I asked about the reasons she had ended up in the hospital.

"The experts here say I had a myocardial infarction," Sarah said. "To us mere mortals, that means I had a heart attack."

She always struck me as someone who was energic and fit, so I asked about what might have led to her heart condition.

"Dave, I love my job and thoroughly enjoy the people I work with," she told me. "But I know what you know—the company is nonstop pressure and demands. It can be a treadmill at full speed. This health crisis is a wake-up call. I've endured chronic stress for years and have not taken care of myself. And now here I am, sitting in a hospital bed."

I asked her to share more, if she wanted to.

"For years," she continued, "I've felt like I couldn't ask for help because I didn't want to let management down or seem incapable. I always wanted to meet the expectations and get a good annual review."

By "management," I knew I was one of the people she was referring to, among other higher-ups.

Hearing this, I was hit with a wave of guilt. Here was someone who had given so much of herself to the company, yet I had never taken the time to show her that I cared about her beyond her work role.

> **Loving the people you lead is not just a leadership tactic—it is a fundamental principle that transforms both leaders and their teams.**

After leaving the hospital, I couldn't stop thinking about about our conversation. I realized that in my pursuit of success, I had overlooked the most critical aspect of leadership—caring for the people who make that success possible. I had been so focused on the mechanics of running a company that I had forgotten about the hearts and minds of the people working beside me.

The next day, I called a meeting with my leadership team, but this time it wasn't about metrics or budgets. I started by apologizing for being so distant and out of touch. I told them about my visit to Sarah and how it opened my eyes to the importance of showing genuine care and love for each team member. I asked each of them to prioritize the well-being of their teams and to lead with empathy and compassion.

A WAKE-UP CALL FOR ME

From that day forward, I made a conscious effort to change my approach to leadership. I began spending time with my employees, not just as a boss but as a colleague who cared about their lives and their well-being. I started holding regular one-on-one meetings where we talked about more than just work—we discussed their goals, their families, and their challenges. I encouraged a culture where people felt comfortable coming to me or their managers with any issues, knowing they would be met with understanding and support.

The changes didn't happen overnight, but slowly the atmosphere in the office began to shift. People were more engaged, more connected, and turnover decreased significantly. Our productivity didn't suffer—in fact, it improved, because when people feel valued and supported, they are more motivated to give their best.

Looking back, I see how much I had to learn about leadership. And I am so glad that experience with Sarah—and similar experiences—came early in my career and prompted a significant shift in how I viewed the people I had the privilege of leading.

I learned that effective leadership is not just about driving results; it's about caring for the people who make those results possible. Loving and caring for your team isn't a distraction from the goals—it's what makes achieving those goals sustainable. The company and the team I led went on to be highly successful and profitable. That was due to wise business strategies, but mostly because the people working there—from top to bottom—felt cared for, protected, and nurtured. It's not hyperbole to say they felt loved.

THE IMPORTANCE OF LEADING WITH LOVE

Loving the people you lead is a powerful force that transcends traditional leadership practices and has a profound impact on both individuals and organizations. At its core, love in leadership is about genuinely caring for the well-being of each person on your team. It's about seeing them as more than just employees or colleagues, but also as unique individuals with their own hopes, dreams, and challenges.

When leaders embrace this perspective, they create an environment where people feel valued, understood, and supported.

One of the most significant outcomes of loving leadership is the development of deep trust between leaders and their teams. Trust is the bedrock of any successful organization, and it is built when leaders consistently demonstrate care and concern for their people. When team members know that their leader genuinely loves and values them, they are more likely to be open, honest, and engaged in their work. This trust leads to greater collaboration, innovation, and a willingness to go the extra mile for the team and the organization.

> When leaders choose to lead with love, they cultivate empathy, patience, and humility—qualities that are essential for personal growth and development.

Moreover, loving the people you lead fosters a sense of belonging and purpose within the team. People want to feel that they are part of something bigger than themselves, that their work matters, and that they are contributing to a meaningful cause. A leader who shows love creates a culture where individuals are motivated not just by external rewards but also by a deep sense of connection and commitment to the team and its goals. This sense of belonging enhances job satisfaction, reduces turnover, and leads to higher levels of performance and productivity.

Loving leadership also has a transformative impact on leaders themselves. When leaders choose to lead with love, they cultivate empathy, patience, and humility—qualities that are essential for personal growth and development. Leading with love requires leaders to put aside their egos, listen actively, and prioritize the needs of others. This self-less approach to leadership not only benefits the team but also enriches the leader's own life, leading to deeper, more fulfilling relationships both in and out of the workplace.

JESUS: THE ULTIMATE EXAMPLE OF LOVING LEADERSHIP

For leaders with a faith perspective, the ultimate example of how to love the people we lead is found in Jesus Christ. Jesus not only preached about love but consistently demonstrated it in his interactions with those he led—his disciples and the broader community. His leadership was rooted in profound love, compassion, and humility, setting a standard that transcends time and culture.

One of the most powerful examples of Jesus' loving leadership is found in John 13, where he washes the feet of his disciples. This act of service, typically performed by the lowest servant, demonstrated Jesus' humility and deep love for those he led. By kneeling before his disciples and performing this humble task, Jesus showed that true leadership is not about exerting power or authority but about serving others with love. He told them, "I have set you an example that you should do as I have done for you" (John 13:15). This act of love and service illustrated that leadership is a call to selflessness and a commitment to the well-being of those we lead.

Another example is found in Jesus' interaction with Peter after Jesus' resurrection. Despite Peter's denial of Jesus three times, Jesus did not respond with anger or condemnation. Instead, he lovingly restored Peter, asking him three times, "Do you love me?" and then entrusting him with the care of his flock, i.e., his people (John 21:15–17). This encounter highlights Jesus' forgiving and restorative love, demonstrating that loving leaders do not hold grudges but instead seek to restore and uplift those who falter.

What's more, throughout his ministry Jesus consistently showed compassion to those who were marginalized, ill, or in need. He healed the sick, fed the hungry, and comforted the sorrowful, always putting the needs of others before his own. This compassionate love is a powerful example for leaders today, reminding us that our primary responsibility is to care for the people we lead, especially in their times of need.

PRACTICAL STEPS FOR LOVING THE PEOPLE YOU LEAD

After my experience with Sarah, I sought to learn how to genuinely and practically show love to the people I led. Here are some of the ways I learned to put heartfelt care into daily practice:

Listen actively. One of the most tangible ways to show love to your team is by listening closely and carefully. This means being fully present in conversations, seeking to understand before being understood, and valuing their opinions and feelings. Active listening demonstrates respect and shows that you care about their thoughts and concerns.

Invest in the growth of your team members. Love in leadership is also about helping people reach their full potential. Provide opportunities for professional development, mentorship, and coaching. Encourage continuous learning, and celebrate their achievements. By investing in their growth, you show that you care about their future and believe in their abilities.

Strive to be consistently compassionate. Compassion is a critical aspect of loving leadership. Understand that your team members are human beings with emotions, challenges, and personal lives. Be there for them in times of need, offer support when they face difficulties, and create a compassionate environment where people feel comfortable being themselves.

Recognize and appreciate. Regularly acknowledge the hard work and contributions of your team members. Public recognition and private appreciation go a long way in making people feel valued and loved. Tailor your recognition to individual preferences—some may appreciate a public shout-out, while others may prefer a handwritten note.

Lead by example. Demonstrate love through your actions. Show humility, fairness, and integrity in your decisions. Be a role model in treating others with kindness and respect. When your team sees you leading with love, they are more likely to mirror those behaviors in their interactions with others.

Build genuine relationships. Take the time to know your team members beyond their professional roles. Learn about their interests, families, and aspirations. Building genuine relationships fosters trust and makes people feel truly valued. This personal connection enhances teamwork and collaboration.

Communicate transparently. Love also manifests in honesty and transparency. Keep your team informed about organizational changes, decisions, and expectations. Open and honest communication builds trust and shows that you respect them enough to share important information.

Be patient and forgiving. People make mistakes, and loving leaders are patient and forgiving. Instead of harshly criticizing errors, use them as learning opportunities. Offer guidance and support to help team members improve, and be patient as they grow and develop.

LOVE IS NOT A "TO-DO" ITEM ON YOUR LIST

Loving the people you lead is not just a leadership tactic—it is a fundamental principle that transforms both leaders and their teams. It fosters deep trust, a sense of belonging, and a commitment to shared goals that drives both personal and organizational success.

Jesus, the ultimate example of loving leadership, demonstrated through his life and ministry how true leadership is rooted in love, service, and compassion. By following his example—actively listening, investing in others, showing compassion, and leading by example—leaders today can cultivate a culture of love that transcends traditional leadership metrics and creates a thriving, connected community. Love in leadership is about more than achieving goals—it's about building a community where everyone can flourish and contribute their best.

9

Go to God for Guidance

Prayer lifts you and your team.

Over my years of corporate leadership, I developed a solid belief in a private practice that may come as a surprise.

You won't come across it in most MBA classes or leadership books. I kind of drifted into this practice on my own, only to wonder how I ever led people successfully without it. In the years since, I've found it vital to leading my people effectively—and ultimately to team and corporate success.

What on Earth could I be talking about?

I'm talking about prayer. This involves having regular, heartfelt conversations with God about yourself, your people, and your enterprise. It will help make you a better leader. Not only that, but it will make you a better all-around *person*. Take it from one who's been there, done that.

Leadership author John C. Maxwell agrees: "Every time I've had a breakthrough in my life, it was because of prayer." Sir William Gurney Benhem, the British author and longtime mayor from long ago, is famous for stating, "He who ceases to pray ceases to prosper."

As I led people and companies, I found these sentiments to be resoundingly true. Praying regularly for personal wisdom, for your team, and for your company's favor puts

"In God We Trust" into action. In times of uncertainty or crisis, it can provide clarity and peace. As pastor and author Rick Warren says, "God can handle your doubt, anger, fear, grief, confusion, and questions. You can bring everything to him in prayer."

I respectfully recognize that you may or may not (yet) be comfortable with the idea of praying for your team and your enterprise. That's okay for now. As best-selling author Max Lucado assures us, "Our prayers may be awkward. Our attempts may be feeble. But since the power of prayer is in the One who hears it and not in the one who says it, our prayers do make a difference."

> Our Creator invites us—in fact, *urges* us—to seek his help in being exemplary leaders.

So come along with me as I highlight three ideas that I've found helpful when it comes to prayer. If you approach them with an open mind and heart, I'm confident they just might upgrade the effectiveness of your leadership and your life.

MAKE SURE YOUR OWN HEART IS RIGHT

First and foremost, a good leader must be sure his or her heart is in the right place throughout the workday. This can be challenging when the phone calls and emails and employees at your door pile up, each a potential disruption of your own priorities. But I found that asking God for his guidance as my day began, followed by frequent "quick prayers" throughout the day, greatly helped me greet my people with a caring smile or a word of affirmation or encouragement, and respond to the unexpected with calm confidence.

Our Creator invites us—in fact, *urges* us—to seek his help in being exemplary leaders. He *wants* to empower and enable us. In Jeremiah 33:3 (NKJV), he promises, "Call to Me, and I will answer you, and show you great and mighty things, which you do not know."

Many other Scriptures verify his desire to hear from us and help us keep our hearts right. For starters, let me recommend a brief prayer written by one of history's greatest leaders, King David: "May these words of my mouth and this meditation of my heart be pleasing in your sight, LORD, my Rock and my Redeemer" (Psalm 19:14 NLT). While this is a quick prayer, it's worth some meditation on our part. I find it especially meaningful to contemplate this psalm *from the bottom to the top*. Follow me for the natural progression, and you'll see what I mean.

> **Prayer can be considered an ongoing dialogue with God, a continual conversation with him.**

First (from the bottom of the verse), Psalm 19:14 assumes that the praying leader believes in God as his or her "Rock" and "Redeemer." This means knowing and trusting God personally, as King David did, regarding God as a reliable friend who wants the best for us. "Prayer is not overcoming God's reluctance," said that great reformer of history, Martin Luther. "It is laying hold of His willingness."

Second, we're praying that our thoughts and words will be "pleasing" in God's sight. It expresses both our desire to please him as well as our dependence on him to do so. When we ask him, in faith, he enables us.

Then there's the "meditation of my heart," which means our attitudes and our thoughts. When we're dogged by worry over work, we can take pastor and podcaster Dave Willis's advice: "When you feel like worrying, try praying instead. Worrying only creates more stress, but prayer creates more peace. God is bigger than whatever is stressing you out."

Is my attitude upbeat, calm, positive? Do my thoughts toward others grant them the benefit of the doubt? Praying David's prayer, and meaning it, asks the Lord to guard my attitudes and thoughts—the "meditation of my heart."

Which brings us to "may the words of my mouth." Our words spring from the heart. Negative thoughts breed detrimental words, while upbeat thoughts lead to constructive words. Good leaders keep their thoughts right so they will speak (and write) words of calm confidence, appreciation, and affirmation, no matter the circumstances.

TALK DAILY WITH GOD

God wants to spend time with you. Granted, he is all-knowing and all-seeing, so he is aware of everything about your life before you mention anything to him. But God's eagerness to spend time with you goes beyond you coming to him with a list of requests.

Prayer can be considered an ongoing dialogue with God, a continual conversation with him. Think of prayer as taking a long drive with a family member or close friend. You don't spend every moment talking, yet you remain aware of each other, even connected to each other. You comment on things you see outside the car windows. You make plans about where you're going to stop and what you're going to do. You talk about what you're interested in or spend time asking for insight about a difficult situation. You relish the journey together because of your camaraderie and closeness.

Heartfelt and honest conversation with God is yours for the having. Perhaps best of all, when talking with God, you can ask for wisdom and guidance amid all your struggles. Everyone on Earth could use divine direction and understanding in their daily lives—and this is especially true for those struggling through a tough issue. Prayer is a powerful source of insight and inspiration as you pursue healing forever.

Here are some areas I pray for each day—reminders to me that I would be stuck in my tracks without the guidance of a gracious God to help me find my way. So consider joining me as together we pray for . . .

- Strength to live a courageous life
- A thankful spirit, maintaining gratitude during good times and bad times
- God's power to utilize the talents and passions he has given us
- Wisdom to consistently make choices that show respect for ourselves and others
- Health and healing, asking God to guide us steadily toward strength and comfort in our body, mind, and soul

LISTEN CLOSELY: GOD IS SPEAKING TO YOU

To hear the voice of God, you need to focus on what is being said to you. There is a time to cry out to God, and there is a time to be quiet. Solomon tells us there is "a time to be silent and a time to speak" (Ecclesiastes 3:7). Not surprisingly, silence comes before speaking.

Some people scoff at the idea that God speaks back, but only because they've never heard an audible voice answer them directly. Prayer is a *conversation*—two-way communication. The truth is, God speaks all the time, and we would have no trouble hearing him if we'd only broaden our definition of speech. The psalmist wrote,

> The heavens declare the glory of God;
>   the skies proclaim the work of his hands.
> Day after day they pour forth speech;
>   night after night they reveal knowledge.
> They have no speech, they use no words;
>   no sound is heard from them.
> Yet their voice goes out into all the earth,
>   their words to the ends of the world. (Psalm 19:1–4)

As this psalm so eloquently describes, God certainly speaks through nature. His message is one of majesty and grandeur, to be sure, but also of balance, beauty, and rebirth—qualities we can cling to in perilous times.

That's just the beginning. God's voice can also be heard in art and music, in stories that inspire us to be more and do better. He speaks in every act of kindness, no matter how small. God's part of the conversation is found in sacred Scriptures and in the words of wise people throughout time who've labored to bring light into the darkness of ignorance. God speaks in our dreams and in subtle moments of intuition.

But, like in every conversation, it's possible not to hear a word of it. Why? Because you're not listening. Until you choose to believe God will actually answer your questions and calm your fears, it's likely you'll frantically do all the talking and never make room for his reply. To avoid this unnecessary mistake, slow down, set aside time to be quiet, and extend your awareness. Go looking for the diverse love notes from God scattered around the world—and you will find them.

LIFT UP YOUR PEOPLE

Several years ago I came across an inspiring true story of a publishing CEO who cared deeply for his team. One weekday morning an employee arrived early and found the CEO seated at the employee's desk, his head cradled in one arm—and sound asleep.

I don't know how the early-arriving staff member awakened his CEO. Probably *very* gently! What the CEO confided to him wasn't meant to go further, but inevitably, word got out. This leader, a man of deep faith, had devoted the night to moving from desk to desk throughout the company, then sitting at each employee's desk, and praying for them by name.

I don't presume to know for certain, but I doubt it is mere coincidence that this Christian book publishing house went on to thrive—producing, among many other successful projects, one of world's top-selling Bible translations and the best-selling Christian fiction series of all time.

If we profess faith in God, one of the most caring things we can do for our people is pray for them. It doesn't need to be an all-night vigil—just heartfelt, private prayer for them, regardless of where they may be in their spiritual journey.

How to pray? I suggest taking time every couple of weeks to lift up each teammate by name. What to pray? For God's blessing on them and their labor. For their discernment and diligence. For their attitude, demeanor, and teamwork. For their health and family.

We may or may not see obvious answers right away. But as leadership speaker and author Craig Groeschel aptly puts it, "Your prayer for someone may or may not change them, but it always changes *you*."

LIFT UP YOUR ENTERPRISE

There's a powerful promise in the Scriptures that was given in another time and context but that many God-honoring leaders rightly claim today. "'For I know the plans I have for you,' says the LORD. 'They are plans for good and not for disaster, to give you a future and a hope'" (Jeremiah 29:11 NLT).

For me, this is a cordial invitation to lift up our enterprise for God's guidance and blessing.

When to pray? Early and often. How to pray? For wisdom among leaders and supervisors. That every decision and transaction would be conceived and completed with integrity. For a company-wide "can-do" spirit. For favor in the marketplace and for fiscal success.

AND WHEN WORRIES COME . . .

I'll close with a simple but powerful thought. As leaders, many of our workdays are fraught with stressors and unpleasant surprises. That's to be expected. But we don't have to let worries overwhelm us. Instead, we can heed the timeless advice of Martin Luther: "Pray, and let God worry."

And therein lies the key to calm confidence.

10

Surround Yourself with Top-Notch People

You're only as effective as the team around you.

When I arrived at Torbitt and Castleman as CEO, an established practice had executives and managers share administrative assistants as a cost-saving measure for the company. I've always been a strong proponent of trimming budgets and reining in costs—unless particular belt-tightening tactics proved counterproductive.

In this situation, I proved to be the counterproductive culprit.

It quickly became clear to my team that I severely lacked typing and computer skills. That's not surprising since the only poor grade I got in high school was a D-minus in typing class, and my deficiencies had not improved much since then. And to say that I was not "tech savvy" would be a vast understatement.

Most of my key executives were aware of my limitations when they read my extremely short email responses to their questions and comments. I could hardly type a letter without requiring copious amounts of time. They probably wondered what developing country or off-grid community their new leader had come from. Stepping into my new big role, with so much to do and communicate, I definitely needed someone to come alongside and help me.

One day our general counsel, Don, recommended that Darlene Morris would be an excellent person to become my administrative assistant. After hearing about her outstanding skills and experience, I talked with her to see if she would be a good fit, the one to make up for my shortcomings. She turned out to be as sharp and motivated as advertised, so I quickly invited her to join our team.

> Leaders who surround themselves with top-notch people demonstrate humility— the recognition that you don't have all the answers and that others have strengths you do not possess.

Darlene dived into her new duties, cheerfully and skillfully helping me with the dozens of details I needed to attend to every day. She not only handled all the "grunt work" and mundane tasks that fall on an admin; she also offered creative ideas, provided insight into office problems, and helped to streamline our systems.

Most of all, she kept me on task and on schedule—not always an easy job.

Every Friday morning, I held a meeting with key staff members to better understand the challenges and opportunities throughout the company. After a few weeks, I felt the Friday meetings were going well, as I was getting acquainted with my team and learning the intricacies of the company's inner workings.

But I soon found out that my right-hand specialist, Darlene, did not share my positive perspective on these meetings.

"Dave," she told me, graciously but firmly, "these meetings consistently run long, far beyond the scheduled time frame. That creates a domino effect for the rest of the day. I have to reschedule all of your other appointments, and sometimes meetings have to be canceled altogether. The train gets derailed first thing in the morning and then never gets back on track."

"I hear what you are saying, and I can see how this is causing you headaches," I responded. "Plus, it's disruptive to other people's schedules, which isn't fair. I'll do everything I can to keep these meetings on schedule. I mean it, boss."

She chuckled and said she would hold me to it.

And she needed to, because doing "everything I can" proved insufficient. The morning meetings continued to go over schedule and throw off the rest of the day.

Darlene decided to step up her enforcement. With her typical sense of humor—while clearly getting her message across—she arranged the conference room for the next meeting with an unspoken warning to me. On the table in front of my chair, she placed a picture of a scowling nun wearing a habit and holding a ruler.

Darline was a devout Roman Catholic and knew I had attended a strict Catholic elementary school as a boy. On several occasions, I had been whacked on the knuckles by one of the nuns for talking in class or passing notes to a friend. So Darlene's picture carried weight with me! I knew Darlene was serious and became afraid that she, too, might whack my knuckles with a ruler.

Her message did indeed get across. Thereafter, I made absolutely sure the meetings didn't go overtime, and they never did.

This is just one example of Darlene's extraordinary skill at managing an office . . . which mostly meant managing people . . . which mostly meant managing me. I began to call her Sister Mary Darlene (SMD for short) for her blend of deep faith, dedication, and conscientious work ethic. It was a good-natured honorary title that she appreciated.

"Sister Mary Darlene," I sometimes said to her, "I don't care what your official job title is, we might as well call you co-CEO. I'm sure I could sneak off for a month's vacation, and you would keep the place humming along as usual."

"I bet I could," she'd say, "but you know I wouldn't let you. After all, I've got my ruler right here."

WE'RE NOTHING WITHOUT OUR TEAMMATES

It is often said that leaders are only as good as the team they lead, and this statement couldn't be more accurate. A great leader understands that success is not a solo venture—it is the product of collaboration, collective ideas, and shared passion.

Surrounding yourself with top-notch people creates a ripple effect. When your team is made up of high-caliber individuals, their excellence and dedication have a cascading influence on the organization. They raise the bar for everyone, establishing a culture of excellence, accountability, and growth. The best people inspire others to be their best selves, which leads to continuous improvement and sustained success.

Top-notch people bring more than just skills and experience; they offer a collective brainpower that is greater than the sum of its parts. Each person sees the world through a unique lens shaped by their background, experiences, and expertise. When combined, these diverse perspectives create a wealth of knowledge that enriches decision-making.

A leader who taps into this collective creativity and intelligence is less likely to make shortsighted or uninformed choices. The strength of a team lies in its diversity, and the more varied the perspectives, the stronger the collective wisdom becomes.

EMPOWERMENT AND GROWTH

Top-notch people don't just enhance your leadership—they push you to grow. When you surround yourself with individuals who are experts in their fields, you have the opportunity to learn from them. They challenge you to think differently, expand your knowledge, and continuously improve as a leader.

I love the story found in Exodus 18, where we see Moses receiving advice from his father-in-law, Jethro, about the importance of delegation. Moses was trying to do everything himself, but Jethro observed, "The work is too heavy for you; you cannot handle it alone" (Exodus 18:18). He advised Moses to appoint capable men to share the load. By surrounding himself with skilled leaders, Moses not only eased his burden but also empowered others to lead and grow.

Leaders who surround themselves with top-notch people demonstrate humility—the recognition that you don't have all the answers and that others have strengths you do not possess. This humility opens the door to empowerment. By delegating responsibility to competent individuals, you create an environment where people feel valued and trusted. This, in turn, leads to higher morale, greater ownership, and a stronger overall team.

CHOOSING THE RIGHT PEOPLE

Surrounding yourself with top-notch people starts with choosing the right individuals. This process requires discernment, wisdom, and sometimes patience. It's not enough to look for individuals with impressive résumés or the right credentials. You must seek out people who align with your values, share your vision, and possess the character to make tough decisions in challenging situations.

Jesus himself modeled this when choosing his twelve disciples. He didn't pick the most educated or influential individuals of the time. Instead, he selected people from all walks of life—fishermen, tax collectors, and zealots. What mattered most to Jesus was not their past but their willingness to learn, grow, and serve a greater purpose. As a leader, you must be intentional about selecting people who have not only the skills and expertise but also the heart to grow and contribute meaningfully.

The legacy of a leader is often defined by the people they lead. Leaders who surround themselves with top-notch individuals are more likely to leave a lasting impact. These people will not only carry the leader's vision forward but also build upon it, creating a ripple effect that influences future generations.

THE QUALITIES FOUND IN TOP-NOTCH PEOPLE

What are the specific qualities you should seek in these top-notch individuals? Identifying the right traits can ensure that you are building a team of capable, trustworthy, and driven people who will help you succeed in your mission. Here are some key qualities to look for when selecting top-notch people:

Character and integrity. Integrity is nonnegotiable when building a team of high-performing individuals. People with strong character do the right thing, even when no one is watching. They stand firm in their values, uphold ethical standards, and act with honesty and transparency. As Proverbs 10:9 says, "Whoever walks in integrity walks securely, but whoever takes crooked paths will be found out." Individuals with integrity create an atmosphere of trust, which is the foundation of a successful team.

> A positive mind-set allows top-notch people to focus on solutions rather than problems, lifting the morale of those around them and contributing to a healthy, productive work environment.

A person's character influences how they handle challenges, respond to pressure, and interact with others. You want to surround yourself with people who exhibit reliability, trustworthiness, and consistency in their actions. These are the types of individuals you can count on to make decisions in the best interest of the team and the organization, even when faced with difficult choices.

Work ethic and commitment. A strong work ethic sets top performers apart from the rest. Look for people who demonstrate a commitment to excellence and a willingness to go above and beyond what is expected. These individuals take ownership of their responsibilities, meet deadlines, and consistently produce high-quality work. They are not satisfied with mediocrity and are driven by a desire to achieve the best possible results.

In Colossians 3:23, the Bible tells us, "Whatever you do, do it heartily, as to the Lord and not to men" (NKJV). Top-notch people approach their work with diligence and passion, knowing that their efforts have a higher purpose. They are dedicated to the mission and vision of the organization and are willing to put in the time and energy required to succeed.

Humility and willingness to learn. Humility is an often-overlooked trait, but it is a hallmark of truly great individuals. Humble people understand that they don't have all the answers, and they are open to learning from others. They are willing to receive feedback, admit their mistakes, and grow from their experiences. Humility fosters a culture of continuous improvement, as individuals are not afraid to acknowledge their weaknesses and seek opportunities for development.

Top-notch people are lifelong learners. They are curious, eager to expand their knowledge, and always looking for ways to improve themselves. A humble, teachable spirit ensures that these individuals will not rest on their laurels but will continue to evolve and grow, bringing even greater value to the team over time.

Collaboration and team spirit. No matter how talented an individual may be, they must be able to work well with others to contribute to a high-functioning team. Collaboration is essential for achieving collective success. Top-notch people are team players who prioritize the success of the group over their individual achievements. They are generous with their knowledge, willing to help others, and thrive in environments where people work together toward a common goal.

In Ecclesiastes 4:9–10, we read, "Two are better than one, because they have a good return for their labor: If either of them falls down, one can help the other up." Top-performing individuals understand the value of teamwork and know that they can accomplish far more when working together than they could on their own.

Resilience and grit. The path to success is rarely smooth. Leaders need individuals who can weather storms and bounce back from setbacks with determination and resilience. Resilient people possess grit—they don't give up easily, even in the face of adversity. They remain focused on the long-term goals and are willing to push through challenges to achieve them.

Resilience is an invaluable trait in times of uncertainty or difficulty. Top-notch people understand that setbacks are part of the journey and use those experiences to learn and grow stronger. As James 1:2–3 says, "Consider it pure joy, my brothers and sisters, whenever you face trials of many kinds, because you know that the testing of your faith produces perseverance." A resilient team will stand firm and continue to push forward, no matter what obstacles arise.

Adaptability and flexibility. In today's rapidly changing world, adaptability is essential. Top performers are flexible and open to change, able to pivot when necessary and embrace new ideas or technologies. They thrive in dynamic environments and are not daunted by shifting priorities or unexpected challenges.

Leaders who surround themselves with adaptable individuals will have a team that can respond quickly to new opportunities and navigate disruptions with ease. These people are not rigid in their thinking; instead, they are agile and resourceful, able to find creative solutions to problems that arise.

Positive attitude. A positive attitude is contagious. Surrounding yourself with individuals who maintain optimism and enthusiasm, even in tough times, can uplift the entire team. These individuals not only are pleasant to work with but also help create a culture of positivity and encouragement.

In Philippians 4:8, Paul advises, "Whatever is true, whatever is noble, whatever is right, whatever is pure, whatever is lovely, whatever is admirable—if anything is excellent or praiseworthy—think about such things." A positive mind-set allows top-notch people to focus on solutions rather than problems, lifting the morale of those around them and contributing to a healthy, productive work environment.

Every leader should have a Sister Mary Darlene in their life. She came to her role, and our team, equipped and eager to pitch in on any project and solve any problem. She brought with her talents that I didn't possess, freeing me to do all of the tasks I did best and handling all of the situations where I fell short. That's what I mean about surrounding ourselves with top-notch people!

When leaders surround themselves with top-notch people who possess the qualities I mentioned, they set their teams—and themselves—on a path to excellence. The individuals you choose to have around you will either lift you higher or hold you back, and the right people can elevate your leadership, enhance your vision, and create a culture of success that endures for years to come. Seek out those who embody character, competence, humility, and resilience, and you will be well on your way to building a team that can achieve great things.

11

Optimize Your Optimism

Your enthusiasm and hopefulness are contagious.

At age fifty-five, I thought I had seen it all. I'd spent over thirty years as an executive in the corporate world, and I'd led teams through every kind of storm—mergers, market downturns, rapid growth. But as I sat in my office one afternoon, looking out at the city skyline, something felt wrong.

On paper, the company I was with at the time was doing well—hitting revenue targets, acquiring new clients, delivering projects on time—but the energy was gone. The spark that used to drive my team had dulled. I could see it in their faces, hear it in the monotony of our meetings. Morale had plummeted, and I didn't know why.

I tried everything to fix it. Employee surveys, team-building exercises, even reorganizing departments to spark some life back into the company. But nothing worked. Productivity stayed steady, but there was no excitement, no drive. I could feel it weighing on me too. I started to wonder if the team was burning out—or if I was the problem.

After another uninspired all-hands meeting, I reached out to my former boss and unofficial mentor Bill Savel, a leadership genius if ever I've met one. I had known Bill for years, and he always had a way of cutting through the noise to pinpoint the real issue. As we sat down together at a coffee shop near my office, I laid everything out.

"Bill, I can't figure it out. The company's doing well, but there's no energy left in the team. We're just going through the motions. I've tried everything—team lunches, incentives, even restructuring—but nothing's getting people excited again."

I shared much more as Bill listened quietly, nodding and jotting some notes. Then he looked me straight in the eye.

> When people believe in the future, they are more willing to invest themselves fully in the present.

"Dave," he said, "I'm going to ask you something important. How's your energy and optimism these days?"

That question stopped me cold. "My energy and optimism?" I asked, a bit confused.

"Yeah," he said, leaning forward. "You've always been a high-energy, optimistic leader. You're the kind of guy who people follow because they feed off your enthusiasm. But right now, it sounds like you're going through the motions too. What kind of emotional energy are you bringing to the office every day? How do you feel when you walk into that building?"

Honestly, I hadn't thought about it. But now that he'd asked, I realized something: I hadn't been feeling hopeful and enthusiastic myself. I'd been stressed, maybe a little burned out, focusing too much on the numbers and not enough on why I'd taken this journey in the first place. I'd lost that spark, and I hadn't even noticed.

Bill continued, "You've built a strong team, Dave. They know how to do their jobs. What they need now is for you to show up with energy, with optimism. If you want morale to improve, you need to improve your own attitude first. You set the tone for the company. If you're not excited, why should they be?"

I sat back, thinking about what he'd said. He was right. I'd been so wrapped up in the day-to-day grind that I'd stopped bringing my usual exuberance and excitement for the future, which were exactly what my team needed. I felt drained, and it was rubbing off on them.

"So what do I do?" I asked, feeling a bit at a loss.

"Start with yourself," Bill said simply. "Get back in touch with why you love what you do. Find that optimism again, and bring it into the office every day. When you walk in, don't just look at the numbers—look at the people. Talk to them. Spread that energy. The team will pick up on it."

The next morning, I took Bill's advice to heart. Instead of diving straight into emails or financial reports when I got to the office, I took a moment to reflect. Why had I started this journey? What excited me about leading this company? I reminded myself of the impact we were making, the innovations we were driving.

Then I made it a point to walk through the office with a smile. I greeted people, asked about their weekends, checked in with my managers. When I led meetings, I focused on celebrating the small wins, talking about our long-term vision instead of just the numbers. I wanted the team to remember why we were here and what we were working toward.

It didn't happen overnight, but over the next few weeks, I noticed changes. People started engaging more. Conversations that had been short and transactional now included excitement about new ideas. I saw more smiles, more collaboration, and more energy throughout the workplace. The team was responding to the shift I had made in myself.

One afternoon, one of my senior managers stopped by my office.

"I don't know what's changed, but things feel different around here lately," she said. "People are more engaged, and honestly, I think it's because you've been more positive. It's making a difference."

That comment hit home. Bill had been right—it wasn't the team's morale that needed fixing—it was mine. By reigniting my own optimism, I'd created a ripple effect across the company. I hadn't realized how much my attitude, my energy, and my outlook influenced the entire team.

From that point on, I made it a priority to lead with optimism. I didn't ignore the challenges we faced or sugarcoat difficulties, but I approached them with a mind-set of hope and possibility. And in doing so, I saw how my renewed energy reignited the spark in my team. I learned that leadership isn't just about solving external problems—it's about showing up with the right attitude, leading with enthusiasm, and spreading that energy to everyone around you.

THE UPSIDE OF AN UPBEAT ATTITUDE

We've all heard the cliché that optimists see the glass as half full and pessimists see the glass as half empty. Another adage tells us that optimists see the doughnut and pessimists see the hole.

Whatever your preferred metaphor, we can agree that it is always more enjoyable to spend time around positive, upbeat people rather than negative, downbeat people. What's more, we know that an optimistic outlook has a wide range of benefits. Developing a hopeful attitude is far more potent for wellness than many people recognize.

During the past decades, dozens of research studies have demonstrated the benefits of optimism in individual lives, relationships, organizations, and society as a whole. These studies show that optimists fare better than pessimists at work, in school, and in sports. Positive people are likely to achieve more goals, handle stress more wisely, overcome depression more quickly, cope with illness, and live longer.

Consider just a few specific benefits of optimism:

- An optimistic outlook early in life can predict better health and a lower rate of death during follow-up periods of fifteen to forty years.[2]
- An analysis of fifteen studies involving more than two hundred thousand participants found a 35 percent lower chance of getting heart disease and a 14 percent lower chance of early death for optimistic people.[3]
- Being optimistic has been shown to improve biological risk factors such as high blood sugar and cholesterol.[4]
- Positive thinking boosts immunity and reduces the chance of infection and cancer.[5]
- Even after considering other healthy behaviors, optimistic people had a 15 percent longer life span and 50 percent greater chance of living past eighty-five than people with a negative outlook.[6]

THE EXPECTATION ADVANTAGE

One reason optimists thrive is because they *expect* good things to happen and anticipate a positive outcome for any situation. What a person expects has a significant influence on the final result of whatever their expectations are about.

Researchers often use the twelve-item Life Orientation Test to measure individuals' level of optimism vs. pessimism.[7] This and other tools help to explain that pessimists tend to assume blame for bad events ("It's my fault"), believe the negative situation will continue ("This is going to last forever"), and take on a gloom-and-doom perspective ("This will lead to catastrophe").

In contrast, optimists do not blame themselves for negative events. Instead, they tend to give themselves appropriate credit for good news, believe positive developments will continue on, and remain confident that encouraging events will spill over into many areas of life. Anticipating a positive outcome often becomes a "self-fulfilling prophecy," where a person's actions and attitudes are activated to achieve the desired results.

OPTIMISM IS A MATTER OF OUTLOOK

Can a person who isn't naturally optimistic develop a more positive outlook? Absolutely. Optimism isn't just something a person is born with; optimism can be exercised and strengthened, like a muscle.

One study from 2015 examined the psychological traits of identical twins and found that genetics accounted for 38 percent of optimistic tendencies.[8] An earlier study demonstrated that 20 percent of optimistic outlook is attributed to inherited DNA.[9] Although we would all love to be born with the "optimism gene," these and similar studies should come as good news: optimism is mostly a learned trait, and we can all grow in our ability to become more optimistic.

Most of all, both optimism and pessimism are determined by how we think about our circumstances and adversities. Take Jack, for example. His car broke down on the way to work. Immediately, his mind started swirling with pessimistic views. He thought to himself, *If I weren't so irresponsible, this wouldn't have happened. I should've been more prepared.* Jack believed his entire day would be ruined because of this one setback. And since Jack kept on chastising himself and blaming his "usual bad luck," he did indeed have a lousy day.

> **Optimism in leadership isn't just about maintaining a cheerful disposition—it's about fostering resilience, inspiring others, and driving momentum.**

Now consider Jill, whose car also broke down on the way to work that very same morning. Jill accepts that sometimes difficult things occur that are beyond her control, and she doesn't allow setbacks to negatively impact how she views herself. After inspecting her flat tire, Jill thought to herself, *Well, these things happen. It's no big deal. I'll call a tow truck and catch a ride into work.* Jill accepted the situation, dealt with it, and moved on with her day. She wasn't thrilled with the hassle and coming repair costs, but she kept the predicament in perspective and made a conscious choice to remain positive.

MORE THAN "HAPPY THOUGHTS"

Optimism is a way of reframing obstacles. Here are several strategies for strengthening your optimism muscle:

Practice gratitude, for big things and small things. Spend a few minutes each day listing three blessings in your life and describe how you are enriched by them. Naming the things you're thankful for each day will prompt you to see more and more things to be grateful for. Soon enough, your mind will naturally look for reasons to be grateful.

Look for opportunities in setbacks. Part of what makes a difficult situation so hard to handle is the sense that you are powerless, but that is rarely (if ever) the case. If you suddenly remember something you did or said that offended someone, you now have the opportunity to practice humility and seek forgiveness. If you started a business that did not succeed, you have the opportunity to examine what went wrong so you have a better chance of success next time.

Monitor your self-talk. We talk to ourselves all day long, and the way we talk to ourselves matters tremendously. Our inner voice impacts the atmosphere in our minds, how we view ourselves, and how we perceive the world around us. The way you talk to yourself sets the tone for how you'll engage with the world and the types of interactions you'll come to expect with others.

Dump the drainers. Life is full of people, obligations, and tasks that siphon off our energy and drag us down. Some we can't avoid—but some we can and should. Steer clear of people who soak up your positive energy like a dry sponge in a puddle of water. Likewise, avoid chronic complainers and persistent pessimists.

Pinpoint positives. In your journal—or in conversation with a friend or mentor—identify specific aspects of your life that you feel especially positive and optimistic about. It might be your work, parenting, marriage, spiritual growth, or creative pursuits. Be as specific as possible, and celebrate the good things in your life.

Take an action to demonstrate new thinking. On a piece of paper, write down a negative belief you feel is holding you back and weighing you down. Now take the piece of paper, fold it up, and throw it in your blazing fireplace (or flush it down the toilet, or put it through your shredder). As you do, say to yourself, *This belief has been with me for a long time—but not anymore. I am choosing to let it go and replace it with a more positive, more accurate belief about myself.*

Envision your best possible self and life. For the next two weeks, spend fifteen minutes thinking about and writing about enjoying the best possible circumstances in your future. Ponder your goals and dreams—and envision that everything works out to be the very best situation. Then spend another five minutes visualizing this best future life as vividly as you can, with lots of details. This exercise is more than just a feel-good pep talk for yourself; you will be retraining your mind and redirecting your thoughts. A study published in the *Journal of Behavior Therapy and Experimental Psychiatry* demonstrated that this exercise boosted the participants' level of optimism.[10]

A BOOST IN ORGANIZATIONAL OPTIMISM

A leader's outlook has a direct impact on the morale and performance of their team. When leaders approach challenges with a positive mind-set, they inspire confidence in those around them. Optimism fuels hope, which is essential when navigating uncertainty. Whether during times of growth or adversity, a leader's belief in a positive outcome can shift the entire atmosphere of an organization. This belief doesn't mean ignoring difficulties or glossing over obstacles, but it reflects the conviction that problems are solvable and that tomorrow holds potential.

Optimistic leaders foster a culture of possibility. They encourage their teams to see beyond limitations, focusing on solutions rather than setbacks. By promoting a forward-thinking attitude, they open the door to creativity and innovation. Teams under optimistic leadership are more likely to take risks, think outside the box, and persist through challenges because they trust in the leader's vision. When people believe in the future, they are more willing to invest themselves fully in the present.

Optimism in leadership isn't just about maintaining a cheerful disposition—it's about fostering resilience, inspiring others, and driving momentum. Leaders who believe in a better future, and communicate that belief effectively, create environments where teams feel empowered to push boundaries and achieve more than they thought possible.

12

Compliment Consistently

Recognize the power of praise and affirmation.

I still remember the occasion as if it were yesterday. As a department leader, I was responsible for a team of fifteen men and women, and I reported to our division's vice president. My people seemed responsive to my leadership; their spirit and performance were good. And apparently our productivity was not going unnoticed.

"Dave, there's something I want to tell you," my division leader said one day, when we crossed paths in the hallway. He pulled me into an empty conference room, and we remained standing for a quick, impromptu meeting.

"I've been watching you and your team," he said, smiling. "I want to commend you on how you're leading them. They're meeting or surpassing their goals, and their morale always seems so upbeat. You're doing a great job with them . . . and I'm so glad you're on my team."

At that moment, I felt a lump in my throat. All I could do was smile back and utter a lame, "Well, thanks. I'm glad I'm on your team too." I returned to my office and closed the door, savoring a quiet moment to process what my VP had just said.

A wonderful blend of sensations stirred within me. Wow. I felt suddenly buoyed and bolstered.

I felt affirmed—recognized for how I led my people and for how well they responded.

I felt appreciated—for my initiative and effort on behalf of my department, division, and organization.

I felt valued—as my boss's partner in making the mission happen.

I felt re-energized to continue fighting the good fight.

That day became a milestone in my career path. From then on, I wanted to follow my boss's example with everyone who reported to me. I wanted to notice my people doing their jobs well and compliment them for it. Not generically, but specifically. Not as a group, but individually—as my boss had done for me.

I wanted to apply the timeless words of King Solomon: "Gracious words are a honeycomb, sweet to the soul and healing to the bones" (Proverbs 16:24), and "Like apples of gold in settings of silver, is a word spoken at the proper time" (Proverbs 25:11 NASB).

My dictionary defines *proper* this way: "In a manner that is appropriate or suitable in the circumstances." Well, that's nice, but kind of dry. For the work environment, I would add "sincere, specific, and commending one's character, work ethic, and performance." My boss's kind words embraced all of these qualities. To me, they were "sweet to the soul" and "like apples of gold in settings of silver." Not only heartening but priceless.

SOLOMON WAS RIGHT AND STILL IS

Since that day, as I've tried to live out Solomon's wisdom with those around me, research has consistently confirmed regarding what I've found to be a profound boost to morale and job performance among my people.

One study, cited in the *International Journal of Business Management,* found that while financial incentives are important, recognition and praise from supervisors have a significant impact on employee engagement and motivation. Employees often view recognition as a key motivator, sometimes even valuing it as much as or more than monetary rewards.[11]

> **Employees often view recognition as a key motivator, sometimes even valuing it as much as or more than monetary rewards.**

Another study, published in the *Journal of Applied Psychology,* emphasizes that employee recognition, including praise from managers, plays a critical role in enhancing job satisfaction and motivation. The study underscores that positive reinforcement and acknowledgment from supervisors can be as effective as financial incentives in fostering a motivated workforce.[12]

Dr. Adam Grant, organizational psychologist at the Wharton School, emphasizes that individuals are more likely to engage in discretionary effort—going beyond the basic requirements of their job—when they feel their contributions are recognized and valued. Dr. Grant's research reveals that employees who receive genuine appreciation for their work are more likely to feel a sense of accomplishment and belonging, which in turn boosts their overall engagement and productivity.[13]

What Solomon declared millennia ago still rings true. As leaders, one of the most effective tools at our disposal is sincere, specific praise. Complimenting and validating our employees not only fosters a positive work environment but also drives performance, loyalty, and overall job satisfaction.

That's why I encourage all of us to make sincere praise a part of our leadership toolbox. But the catch is, there are helpful ways and not-so-helpful ways to offer praise to your team members. The helpful ways are almost always well-received. The not-so-helpful can come across as hollow or disingenuous.

Let's look at how to offer words of affirmation effectively and powerfully.

BE SINCERE AND SPECIFIC

First and foundationally, it's essential that your compliments are sincere and specific, rather than generic. A leader who frequently says "good job" without providing specific feedback as to *why* it was a "good job" may come across as insincere. One manager I knew often ended his emails to staff with, "Thanks for all you do." This caused his people to wonder, *Does he even* know *all I do*? Generic platitudes can actually come across as superficial, leading to a cloud of skepticism among team members.

Sincere, specific praise requires your keen observation and acknowledgment of an employee's *specific contributions and efforts*: "Sally, I really appreciate your good work meeting all those deadlines this month. I know they were challenging, but you did it—and everything looked great! That proposal you created for Intrepid Industries is top-notch. Because of your great work on that, we have an excellent chance of landing that account. You really came through for us."

See how this approach acknowledges Sally's particular efforts and skills? Instead of a superficial "good job," it helps reinforce desired behaviors and affirms Sally's specific value to you and the team.

OFFER COMPLIMENTS THAT ARE CLEAR AND APPROPRIATE

It's unfortunate that, in our culture, many people have been conditioned to be hypersensitive or offended by nearly anything. So it goes without saying, but I'll say it anyway: think through your compliment before you offer it. Make sure your words cannot be misconstrued as having ulterior motives. This is true especially when complimenting the appearance of the opposite sex, but in today's world affirming either gender's appearance could be perceived as inappropriate. Ensure that your praise is respectful and relevant, avoiding comments that could be construed as "crossing the line" in any way.

It's okay to compliment one's appearance in a benign, wholesome manner. It's much better to say "What a beautiful sweater" than "You look very attractive in that sweater." But the far more meaningful approach with both men and women is to affirm character, strengths, talents, and effort. This shifts your focus from how people look or dress to what kind of people they are. Recognizing and commending one's integrity, work ethic, and performance will prove far more authentic than offering superficialities.

MAKE PRAISE PERSONAL

My friend Darren told me a true story that underscores how *not* to give sincere and specific praise. With the best of intentions, a former manager had left a note on Darren's desk praising his job performance and work ethic. Nothing wrong so far. In fact, written notes of commendation are a great way to express affirmation. In fact, the note made Darren's day! Until . . .

At lunch in the break room with some of his coworkers, Darren mentioned that he had received a kind note from their supervisor the previous day and how much he appreciated it. Someone chimed in and said, "I got a note yesterday too." Another person said the same thing, and then another. In fact, everyone in the department had received notes, and all with similar wording!

Good intentions, poor execution. This manager had lit a heartwarming fire only to douse it with an impersonal, watered-down approach.

MAKE PRAISE TIMELY

If you're praising someone for specific accomplishments, do so as soon as possible after the accomplishment. Immediate recognition helps employees make the connection between their actions and the positive feedback you give.

Why let it wait until Kara's next annual review? Why wait at all? Of course you can and should cite Kara's achievements in her annual review, but don't let all that time pass between her accomplishments and your commendation. A prompt affirmation from you will assure Kara that you notice and appreciate her diligence—and it will energize her to keep up the good work.

AFFIRM INDIVIDUALLY

In Darren's story above, we saw how *not* to leave notes of appreciation. At first, Darren felt valued and appreciated, grateful that his boss had singled him out for special praise and affirmation. But in a misguided desire not to leave anyone out, his boss diluted the positive effects he had hoped for.

Here's the better way. Write those notes of appreciation and affirmation, but do so mindfully. Not simultaneously to your whole team, but just to the one or few who deserve special kudos for a project nicely done. Or to a team member you would like to pat on the back for her can-do spirit and diligent work. In good time, you can do the same for others on your team, one or two at a time. But not now. All in good time.

Thoughtful, written kudos on a note card, in your own handwriting (forget texts or emails) can boost morale because you've singled out a person as worthy of your special notice and gratitude. It will work wonders to say, "I just wanted you to know how much I appreciate you," followed by specific character qualities you admire. And instead of your message being watered down via group distribution, it will warm the individual's heart. *My boss knows I do good work. He appreciates me! I feel valued.*

GO PUBLIC WITH PRAISE

If you want to amplify words of praise, accentuate the positives publicly. When the team is together, you could say, "I thought it was awesome that Maya spent the past three weekends volunteering with Habitat for Humanity." Or, "Kudos to Jen and Mike, who nailed that client presentation Tuesday. They gave it excellent thought and effort. The client was impressed, and so was I."

Public praise can bequest recipients with a special level of value and pride. Good pride—the kind that makes them want to work even harder, and smarter, to accomplish even greater things. But a word of caution: avoid overpraising the same people repeatedly. Nearly everyone on your team deserves a public "well done" along the way. So spread the joy over time, and watch what happens.

One tactic I employed occasionally is to begin a team meeting by having each person tell what they most appreciate about the person to their right. As we go around the table, the whole room is uplifted as people give and receive sincere compliments. Often, I've observed others around the table nodding their agreement as a praise is being given. One employee even told me afterward, "I'm going to have my family do this at our Thanksgiving table!"

> As leaders, one of the most effective tools at our disposal is sincere, specific praise.

A doctor who has led medical clinics and delivered leadership lectures nationwide took public praise to an unexpected level. After he had commended a male worker for his upbeat attitude and good work, he composed and mailed a letter *to the worker's wife and family*—unbeknownst to the employee. The letter praised this staff member's cheerful spirit, kindness with patients, and excellence on the job. Perhaps most important, the letter closed with heartfelt thanks to this employee's wife and kids for sharing him with the team he served so well.[14]

Can you imagine the scene once he arrived home?

LIKE APPLES OF GOLD

Yes, Solomon was right. Like apples of gold in settings of silver. That's what a word of praise, properly spoken, feels like. Genuine, heartfelt, specific praise makes people feel rich.

I hope you've received such praise in your life and know how good it feels. And I hope you're now more motivated than ever to share warm, apt words of appreciation and praise with those wonderful folks on your team.

They deserve it.

13

Understand Your Unique Leadership Style

God gave each of us the talents and temperament to be our best.

I sat in my office, staring out at the Seattle skyline, feeling more drained than usual. At age sixty I felt like I had hit a high point of my career. I had joined Coinstar, at the time a company with vast potential but also with serious struggles.

Early in my tenure with the company, I implemented changes that led to growth and expansion. But still, something felt off. Despite our success, things weren't right. Much of the team lacked engagement, many of the practices were counterproductive, and morale seemed low throughout the organization.

Questions about my leadership circled in my head: What should I be doing differently? How could I be a more effective leader? Was I part of the problem?

I reached out to Bill Meyer, a consultant who came highly recommended to me from a former boss. Bill's firm specialized in leadership assessment and development, and he had consulted the top management at Microsoft, Starbucks, and many other leading companies.

In my first sit-down with Bill, I learned immediately that he didn't sugarcoat things. He had a knack for getting to the heart of a problem. If anyone could help me figure out what needed improvement—in the company and especially my leadership style—it was him. Bill's calm, confident presence filled the room as we exchanged pleasantries. He settled into the chair across from me, the sound of distant rain tapping against the windows.

> Leadership is not a one-size-fits-all endeavor.

"Dave, something's clearly on your mind," Bill said, his sharp eyes studying me. "What's going on?"

I exhaled heavily and rubbed my temples. "It's the company, Bill. Coinstar's doing well—revenue is up, we're expanding, we've brought on exceptional new people—but something's not working. I'm getting pressure from the board to accelerate progress ASAP. I'm struggling to motivate some key people who need to be highly motivated to achieve our goals. I've tried different approaches—being more hands-on, stepping back, giving them more say—but nothing clicks."

Bill leaned forward, his gaze steady. "How are you showing up as a leader these days?"

That question caught me off guard. "What do you mean?" I asked, unsure where he was going. "I'm doing what I've always done. I make decisions, delegate, work hard. I've even tried being more democratic, but it doesn't feel right."

A small smile tugged at Bill's lips. "That's what I thought. You're trying to adapt without fully understanding your core leadership style. Do you even know what your natural style is?"

I hesitated. "I don't know, Bill. I've never really thought about it. I just . . . lead. I do what the situation demands."

Bill nodded, understanding. "That's where the issue lies. You've stepped into your latest challenge and opportunity, Coinstar, with a specific set of leadership qualities. But now you're spreading yourself thin, trying to be everything for everyone. Your team senses that inconsistency, and it's causing the disconnect."

I leaned in, trying to grasp what he was getting at. "So what's my leadership style then?"

"Think about when you felt most confident leading," Bill said. "What were you doing? Were you inspiring others with a clear vision, or were you down in the trenches, working side by side with your team?"

I thought back. "I've always been hands-on. I love to get acquainted with everyone I can, from the janitors to the C-suite people. I like being in the mix with my team, but I've also made sure they see the bigger picture—telling them exactly where we're heading."

Bill nodded, his eyes lighting up. "That's it. You're a blend of an organizer leader and a perfectionist leader. You drive your team with vision, but you also build trust by working alongside them. But lately, you've been leading in ways that don't fit your natural style. You've become too distracted by all of the day-to-day minutiae, bogged down in trying to please board members, top clients, and everyone else. And your team feels that shift."

It all started to click in my mind.

"You're right," I responded. "I've been trying so hard to adapt that I've lost sight of what made me an effective leader in the first place."

"That's exactly it," Bill said. "When you lead in ways that don't align with who you are, it shows. Your team picks up on it, and they don't respond the way they used to. Leadership isn't about fitting into a mold—it's about leading with authenticity. When you stick to your natural strengths, your team will follow because they trust your consistency."

I felt a weight lift from my shoulders. "So what should I do next?"

"Start by reflecting on when you were most effective," Bill said. "What were you doing when your team felt most connected to you? Lean into those strengths. You don't need to be everything to everyone. Lead in the way that feels true to you."

> Each leader brings a unique combination of personality traits, experiences, and perspectives to their role.

I leaned back, a sense of relief settling in. "You're right. I've been so focused on adapting to every external pressure that I forgot how I'm wired to lead."

Bill stood up, giving me a reassuring smile. "That's the key, Dave—knowing your strengths and leading from that place. Leadership isn't about doing everything right. It's about understanding yourself and leading with authenticity. Your team craves the real you—the leader who inspires with vision and works alongside them."

As Bill left, the rain had lightened up. And I felt lighter, too, with a renewed sense of direction filling me. I'd been trying to lead by adjusting to external pressures, forgetting my own strengths. Honestly, I had been leading on autopilot, just doing what I'd always done.

Now it was time to get back to leading Coinstar with vision, staying true to myself, and reconnecting with my team. I didn't just need to lead—I needed to lead authentically, and that would make all the difference.

THE IMPORTANCE OF SELF-AWARENESS

Leadership is not a one-size-fits-all endeavor. Each leader brings a unique combination of personality traits, experiences, and perspectives to their role. Understanding and embracing your unique leadership style is essential for leading with authenticity and effectiveness.

As I learned, effective leadership begins with self-awareness. Before you can lead others, you must first understand yourself—your strengths, weaknesses, values, and motivations. Without this foundational knowledge, your leadership will be inconsistent, and you may struggle to align your actions with your vision.

Here are some steps to guide your journey of self-discovery as a leader:

Reflect on past experiences. Analyze situations where you felt most effective as a leader. What were the circumstances? How did you approach problem solving? What feedback did you receive from others? These reflections can reveal patterns in your behavior and decision-making.

Seek feedback from others. Sometimes we are blind to our own strengths and weaknesses. Asking trusted colleagues, mentors, or team members for honest feedback can provide valuable insights into your leadership style. Their perspective can highlight qualities you may not recognize in yourself.

Consider personality and leadership assessments. Tools such as the DiSC, Myers-Briggs Type Indicator (MBTI), or CliftonStrengths can help you identify leadership traits that align with your personality. While these tools are not definitive, they can be a useful starting point for understanding your tendencies in leadership contexts.

After my initial meeting with Bill Meyer, he walked me through the DiSC leadership assessment, which helped enormously in better understanding my unique approach and philosophy. His early perception of my leadership style was spot-on, quickly sizing me up as a "perfectionist" and "organizer" leader. Subsequently, I had all of my key managers and supervisors at Coinstar go through the same assessment, and each told me how helpful it was. The chart on the next page concisely presents the DiSC leadership styles.

EMBRACING YOUR LEADERSHIP STRENGTHS

Once you've identified your core leadership style, the next step is learning to maximize your strengths while addressing potential blind spots. No leadership style is perfect, and every style comes with its own set of challenges. Leaders who can effectively adapt their strengths to fit the needs of their team and organization will find greater success in achieving their goals. Steps forward include these:

Leverage your strengths. Focus on the areas where you naturally excel and use them to your advantage. If you are a transformational leader, for instance, inspire your team by painting a vivid picture of the future. If you are a servant leader, build trust and loyalty by consistently putting your team's needs first.

Address your weaknesses. Every leadership style has potential pitfalls. For example, charismatic leaders may be overly reliant on their charm and neglect necessary details, while transactional leaders may be perceived as rigid or overly focused on rules. Acknowledge these weaknesses and work to mitigate them by seeking complementary skills or delegating tasks to team members who excel in those areas.

DISC TENDENCIES ~ HIGHS AND LOWS

"BEHAVIOR"	DRIVER (D)	SOCIALIZER (I)	ORGANIZER (S)	PERFECTIONIST (C)
HIGHS	Direct/Assertive; Fidgety; Energetic; Self-confident; Strong-willed; Risk-taker	Interactive; Selling; Inspiring; Enthusiastic; Persuasive; Impulsive; Self-promoting; Optimistic; Sociable	Steady; Supportive; Reliable; Stable; Dependable; Consistent; Patient; Sympathetic; Team player	Cautious; Conscientious; Careful; Exacting; Task-oriented; Persistent; Diplomatic; Accurate; Courteous; Tactful
LOWS	Unassuming; Calculated Risk; Self-controlled; Take Charge; Self-critical; Mock-risk-taker	Introverted; Reserved; Observing; Self-controlled; Task-focused; Quiet	Realistic; Integrity; Positive outlook; Humorous; Good-natured; Friendly; Caring	Freely Delegates Details; Uninvolved in Conflicts; Tolerant of Risk/ Uncertainty
"MOTIVATION / NEEDS"				
HIGHS	Action, Results, Control Over Operations; Independence; Opportunities	Applause, Acceptance, Social Recognition; Visibility; Approval; Ideas; Opinions	Stable Work Environment; Appreciation; Recognition; Security; Peaceful Surroundings; Sense of Loyalty	Specific Knowledge of Job; Freedom from Risk of Error; Stable Job; Recognition; Specific Responsibilities; Knowledge-Experts-Work
LOWS	Encouragement; Reassurance; Freedom Over Routine; Autonomy Over Risk Decisions; Higher Authority; Support	Ability to Impress; Work Well Alone; Do not require Team Decision-Making; Peer Approval	Freedom of Expression; Non-Traditional Work Opportunities; Control over Risk/Change; Structured Work Variety; Structured Supervision	Free from Tight Controls; Opportunity for Delegation; Structured Variety; Independent Thinking; Quiet Improvement Change

Be adaptable. A great leader knows when to be flexible. While it's important to lead from your strengths, situations will arise that require different approaches. In some cases, a more directive style may be necessary, while in others, a collaborative approach will be more effective. Adaptability ensures that you can handle the diverse challenges that leadership brings.

THE IMPORTANCE OF IDENTIFYING YOUR UNIQUE LEADERSHIP STYLE

Identifying your unique leadership style is a critical aspect of becoming an effective and impactful leader. Knowing your leadership style helps you lead with clarity, confidence, and consistency. When you understand how you naturally lead, you can leverage your strengths, minimize your weaknesses, and create environments where both you and your team can thrive.

There are several key reasons why identifying your leadership style is important:

Authenticity in leadership. When you know and understand your leadership style, you can lead authentically. Authentic leadership builds trust and credibility because people respond positively to leaders who are genuine and self-aware. Conversely, trying to adopt a style that doesn't align with who you are will likely come across as forced or insincere. Authenticity empowers you to lead with confidence and integrity.

Consistency and clarity. Identifying your leadership style provides clarity for both you and your team. When your team understands your approach to leadership, they know what to expect from you, which leads to greater stability and trust. Consistency in your leadership style helps to set clear expectations and reduces confusion. For example, if your style is collaborative and team-oriented, your team will know that their input is valued and that decision-making will involve collective input.

Alignment with strengths. Understanding your leadership style allows you to focus on your strengths, creating opportunities to lead more effectively. Each leadership style has specific strengths, whether it's inspiring innovation, maintaining order, or fostering collaboration. When you identify your strengths, you can use them to motivate and guide your team more naturally. This self-awareness enables you to play to your strengths while also recognizing areas where you may need support or improvement.

Improved decision-making. Knowing your leadership style gives you insight into how you approach decision-making. Some leaders, like those with a socializer style, prefer to involve others in the process, while others, like transactional leaders, may take a more directive-oriented approach. When you understand your style, you can tailor your decision-making processes to suit the situation while ensuring that your actions align with your core leadership principles.

Better team dynamics. Leaders who are self-aware about their leadership style are better equipped to build strong, cohesive teams. Understanding your own style helps you recognize how to effectively lead different types of individuals within your team. For instance, a transformational leader might focus on inspiring creativity and forward-thinking among team members, while a servant leader will prioritize building trust and empowering others. Your leadership style directly influences the culture of your team, and knowing how to best lead them can foster a more positive, productive environment.

THE POWER OF SELF-AWARENESS IN LEADERSHIP

Understanding your leadership style is essential to leading effectively and authentically. It empowers you to leverage your strengths, improve your decision-making, and engage your team in meaningful ways. Leaders who know their style are better equipped to navigate challenges and adapt to the changing needs of their team. Conversely, leaders who fail to understand their style risk inconsistency, poor team dynamics, and missed opportunities for growth.

To be the best leader you can be, invest time in self-reflection, seek feedback, and commit to continuous learning. Take time to reflect on your leadership journey, listen to those you lead, and never stop developing the gifts God has given you. Your unique leadership style, when aligned with purpose and humility, will create lasting impact and guide others toward success.

Leadership is not about fitting into a predetermined mold or adopting a style that works for someone else. It's about understanding who you are, what drives you, and how you can use your unique talents to lead others effectively. By embracing your authentic leadership style and remaining open to growth and learning, you will find greater fulfillment in your role and inspire others to do the same.

14

Walk in Your
Team Members' Shoes

*There is power in understanding your team's
day-to-day challenges.*

I always considered myself an engaged CEO. I met regularly with my managers, stayed on top of personnel issues, and made sure I understood how each department was doing. I made it my regular practice to walk around the offices, warehouses, and factory floors, talking with anyone I could to better understand their world and how I could lead them. It never made a difference to me if I was talking with a board member or an intern—everyone had value and valuable input.

But when I took over as CEO of Torbitt and Castleman, I quickly realized that some of my upper management team didn't share my perspective that a company is "all for one, and one for all"—a total team effort where the people on the lowest pay grade are just as important as those on the highest pay grade. I saw that some of my top leaders didn't truly understand what life was like for the people on the front lines—the ones actually doing the hard, physical work that kept the company running.

After a very important meeting with the top buyer at Walmart, I brought our executive team together, and we made plans to improve product quality and delivery systems to the retailers. I decided to initiate a new plan I called "Work and Learn," where key management members would work alongside folks on the lower end of the corporate hierarchy, serving for a day in the mail room, the warehouse, the assembly line, or other areas that kept the company running. Members of management wouldn't just shadow and observe; they would work in various departments doing whatever was needed, rolling up their sleeves and getting their hands dirty if necessary. I called for an all-company meeting, gathering hundreds of employees, to explain my plan.

Standing in front of that large crowd, I outlined my new initiative, describing how the plan would work. As I was wrapping up my presentation, I heard a loud voice booming from the back of the room.

"All due respect, sir, but ain't nobody gonna come work with me," said a large man wearing blue coveralls. "No way I can see that happening."

The entire room pivoted to look at this man and then back at me.

"Sir, what's your name?" I asked. "And why do you think no one will come work with you?"

"The name is Yogi, and the work I do is extremely hard and extremely hot. It's just miserable work most of the time. None of y'all want to be there."

The assembled staff stared at me, wondering how I would respond.

"Yogi, how's Thursday of this week?" I said. "I'll be happy to clear my schedule and come work with you all day."

He told me where in the factory he worked and what time he started his shift in the morning.

"Yogi, it's nice to meet you," I replied, "and I'll see you first thing on Thursday."

I imagined that he—and many people in the room—thought I was just calling his bluff and might find some "urgent matter" on Thursday to avoid working with him.

But on Thursday, I made sure to arrive at our meeting spot twenty minutes early, wearing blue coveralls and carrying a lunch pail. Yogi seemed surprised to see me.

> Understanding your team's challenges isn't just a one-time exercise—it should be a regular part of your leadership practice.

I shook his hand and said, "Today, Yogi, you are the boss, and I'm here to learn. And to work."

"Ready for a long day?" Yogi asked, handing me one of the metal paddles they used to stir the chocolate. He had a grin on his face, probably knowing what was coming for me.

"Let's do it," I said, maybe a little too confidently.

Yogi worked in one of the toughest areas of the factory—stirring massive vats of liquid chocolate by hand. The heat in that part of the plant was brutal, with the vats of bubbling chocolate cranking up the humidity to near-unbearable levels. As soon as I walked in, the thick, sweet smell of chocolate mixed with the stifling air hit me like a wall.

For the next few hours, I worked side by side with Yogi, stirring these enormous vats of thick, molten chocolate. What I didn't realize was just how heavy the chocolate was—and how much strength it took to keep stirring without stopping. Sweat poured off me within minutes. My arms ached, my back stiffened, and chocolate frequently splashed out of the vat and onto my clothes.

Meanwhile, Yogi seemed unfazed, accustomed to the hard labor in terrible conditions. At one point, he looked over at me and laughed a little. "Gets to you after a while, huh?"

I wiped my forehead with the back of my arm, which only made things worse since it was already smeared with chocolate.

"It got to me in a hurry," I called out to him. "But, Yogi, you make it look easy compared to my struggles."

He grinned, still stirring. "You get used to it. But it's good for you to see what we're dealing with."

At lunchtime, we sat together, talking as we ate our sandwiches and drank liters of water. I heard about his life at work and beyond work. We talked about our families and the things we liked to do in our free time.

Standing up, ready to trudge back into the sludge, I said, "Yogi, how can you stand these working conditions every day? I've been sweating like I ran a marathon through Death Valley."

"I've asked management many times if we can have a fan in there, just to blow the air around," he explained. "But they've always refused."

"Tomorrow you will have a fan," I assured him. "Count on it."

By the end of the day, I felt completely exhausted. My coveralls were soaked through with sweat, my arms felt like they were made of lead, and I was practically dripping in chocolate. Yogi handed me a towel with a knowing smile, and I couldn't help but laugh at myself. I imagined I looked like the Creature from the Black Lagoon emerging from ooze, or maybe Augustus Gloop, the kid in *Willy Wonka and the Chocolate Factory* who fell into the chocolate river.

"Now you see what it's like up here," Yogi said, not in a confrontational way but with a certain pride.

I nodded, catching my breath. "I've been running this company for a while now, and I never realized just how hard this job is. You guys don't get enough credit for what you do."

WALK A MILE IN THEIR SHOES

As I left the factory that day, chocolate and sweat still clinging to me, I felt something shift inside me. I'd always known our workers were vital to the company, but until I stood in Yogi's shoes, I didn't fully understand what they went through. The experience opened my eyes to how tough their jobs really were and how disconnected many of our key leaders were from the day-to-day challenges they face.

Leading isn't just about big decisions or strategies. It's about getting in the trenches, seeing the work firsthand, and connecting with the people who make everything happen. Leadership is more than giving directions, setting goals, or driving results—it's about building connections and understanding the people you lead.

When leaders take the time to understand the day-to-day challenges their employees face, they create a culture of empathy, trust, and mutual respect.

THE VALUE OF EMPATHY IN LEADERSHIP

Empathy is the cornerstone of effective leadership. It's the ability to understand and share the feelings of others, and in the workplace, it allows leaders to connect with their teams on a deeper level. Walking in the shoes of your team members means going beyond understanding their roles on paper—it means truly seeing the obstacles they face, feeling their frustrations, and recognizing their contributions from their perspective.

A leader who takes the time to listen, observe, and participate in the daily routines of their team gains insights that data or reports alone could never provide. You might discover that the obstacles your employees face are more complex than they seem or that their efforts are going unnoticed because you've been too far removed. By stepping into their world, you demonstrate that you care about their experiences and value their contributions.

> **Leadership is more than giving directions, setting goals, or driving results— it's about building connections and understanding the people you lead.**

Empathy builds trust. When team members see that their leader is invested in understanding their struggles, they feel heard and appreciated. This trust leads to open communication, which is vital for innovation and problem solving. Team members who trust their leaders are more likely to voice concerns, offer feedback, and share ideas, knowing that their perspectives will be valued.

IDENTIFYING AND ADDRESSING CHALLENGES

By walking in your team's shoes, you're better equipped to identify challenges that may be hindering their performance. Often, the true pain points of a job are hidden from leadership because they're lost in layers of middle management or buried under performance reports. Leaders who immerse themselves in the daily tasks of their team can see the friction points firsthand, whether they're caused by inefficient processes, outdated tools, or poor communication.

For example, a leader in a manufacturing company might spend a day working alongside the production line team. In doing so, they might observe that employees are spending valuable time fixing machinery malfunctions or using cumbersome manual processes that could be automated. These kinds of inefficiencies often go unnoticed at the leadership level, but they can have a huge impact on productivity and morale.

Addressing these challenges requires more than just observation—it involves listening to your team. Employees often know exactly what's going wrong and may even have practical solutions, but they don't always feel empowered to share those insights. By engaging directly with their work, you can invite honest feedback and ideas for improvement.

BUILDING A CULTURE OF MUTUAL RESPECT

When leaders take the time to walk in the shoes of their employees, it fosters a culture of mutual respect. Leaders who understand the complexities and challenges of their teams' work are more likely to create policies and make decisions that reflect the realities on the ground. This level of respect goes both ways—employees who feel seen and understood by their leaders are more likely to respect leadership and feel a deeper sense of loyalty to the organization.

A culture of mutual respect also improves collaboration. When leaders demonstrate a willingness to understand the work at every level, it breaks down hierarchies and encourages team members to collaborate openly. Employees feel that their insights and expertise are valued, and leaders benefit from a workforce that is more engaged and willing to contribute to the organization's success.

PRACTICAL WAYS TO WALK IN YOUR TEAM'S SHOES

Understanding your team's challenges isn't just a one-time exercise—it should be a regular part of your leadership practice. Here are some practical ways to walk in the shoes of your team members:

Work alongside them. It's helpful to spend time observing and shadowing your staff; it's even more valuable to work alongside them. This not only helps you understand their work, but it also gives you a chance to see where processes can be improved.

Conduct listening sessions. Hold regular, informal meetings where employees can share their concerns, challenges, and ideas with you directly. Create a safe space where they feel comfortable being honest.

Rotate roles. In larger organizations, leaders can benefit from temporary role rotations, where they take on different responsibilities or spend time in various departments. This crossfunctional exposure helps you see the bigger picture.

Be present on the ground. Regularly visit different departments, locations, or teams, even if it's just to have casual conversations. Open up communication with as many people as you can. The more present you are, the more accessible you'll seem, and the more willing employees will be to share their thoughts.

Engage in hands-on training. Occasionally participate in the same training or onboarding sessions as your employees, especially when new systems or processes are introduced. This will give you insight into how well your organization supports the learning and development of its team members.

A POSTSCRIPT TO THE YOGI STORY

The morning after my day of sweat and toil with Yogi, I headed straight for the head of plant operations. I told him about my day with Yogi and the horrendous working conditions. I said that Yogi had asked several times to get a fan for the scorching work space and his requests had been denied. The plant manager just shrugged and mumbled something.

"Walking into that part of the plant is like walking into hell," I explained, my voice rising with anger. "Tell me why you couldn't get something as simple as a fan, after numerous requests."

He gave lame excuses and acted as if the matter was a big bother and I should not poke my nose into his business.

"Listen," I said, "if we can't get a fan for one of our most hardworking team members, what does that say about us as a company? And what does that say about you as the plant manager?"

He didn't have much to say in reply, so I walked back to my office, made a call to human resources, and began the process immediately to have the plant manager replaced with someone more qualified and caring.

I should also mention that a few of our key leaders refused to participate in our "Work and Learn" program, apparently feeling they were above working alongside people "below" their level. I couldn't fire these individuals due to contractual agreements, but the nonparticipants did not receive their annual bonuses or future promotions that became available.

On a happier note, Yogi and I had developed respect and rapport on our day together to the point that we became friends. Yogi would stop by my office once a week to share with me what was going on in the plant and what was happening in his life. I never considered him an interruption in my day, always welcoming him as a helpful source of information and also an enjoyable friend. In fact, on several occasions Yogi invited me to join him and his friends to shoot guns at the target range. I always had a great time.

Walking in the shoes of your team members is not just an act of empathy; it's a strategic tool for becoming a more effective leader. By understanding the challenges your employees face on a daily basis, you gain insights that help you make better decisions, foster stronger relationships, and build a more collaborative and respectful work environment. When leaders take the time to immerse themselves in their teams' experiences, they create a culture where everyone feels valued, heard, and motivated to contribute to the organization's success.

Most of all, leadership is about people. The more you understand and appreciate their struggles and successes, the more you can lead with empathy, wisdom, and purpose.

15

Disagree Agreeably

*When conflict arises, choose a path to
healthy resolution.*

When I served as COO of Paragon Trade Brands, I
found myself in a situation I hadn't anticipated—a
serious conflict with a colleague I had worked closely with
for several years. Bruce and I had always enjoyed a good
working relationship. We respected each other's expertise
and generally saw eye to eye on most matters.

But as the company began to grow rapidly, our responsibilities increased, and so did the pressure. It was during
one of our strategic planning meetings that things came to
a head.

We were sitting in a conference room with the rest of the
leadership team, discussing the direction of a major project
that was crucial to the company's success. Bruce and I were
presenting our ideas, and it quickly became apparent we
had significantly different approaches. I believed we should
take a more conservative route, given the risks involved,
while Bruce pushed for an aggressive strategy that, in my
opinion, could backfire if things didn't go as planned.

"Look, I get that we need to be cautious," Bruce said, his
voice tinged with frustration, "but we can't afford to play it

safe right now. The market is changing fast, and if we don't take bold steps, we'll fall behind our competitors."

"I understand where you're coming from," I replied, trying to keep my tone calm, "but we're talking about a significant investment here. If this fails, it could set us back for years. We need to think about the long-term stability of the company."

> **Conflict can be a catalyst for growth, innovation, and stronger relationships if handled correctly.**

Bruce shook his head, leaning forward in his chair. "That's exactly the point! If we don't take risks, we won't grow. We've been too conservative for too long. It's time to make a move. C'mon, Dave, this is no time to be passive."

Palpable tension filled the room. The rest of the team watched us, clearly uncomfortable with the disagreement unfolding in front of them. I could feel my frustration rising, and before I knew it, the conversation had escalated.

"You're not listening to what I'm saying," I shot back, more sharply than I intended. "This isn't about being afraid of risks. It's about being smart with our resources. We can't just throw everything at a high-risk strategy and hope it works out!"

Bruce's face hardened. "And you're not seeing the bigger picture! Playing it safe isn't going to get us where we need to go. Dave, if you're so worried about the risks, maybe you're not the right person to lead this project."

The room fell silent. His words hit me like a punch to the gut. I could feel the eyes of the team on me, waiting to see how I would respond. I wanted to fire back, to defend my position, but something stopped me. I realized that this wasn't just about the project—this was about our working relationship, and if we didn't handle this well, it could damage more than just our ability to work together.

As I regularly did in tense moments, I took a deep breath, closed my eyes, and sent up a quick prayer. *God, please give me wisdom in this moment. Help me to handle this situation fairly and honorably.*

Immediately, a Bible verse I'd committed to memory came to mind. Centuries ago, the apostle Paul had written this timeless wisdom: "If it is possible, as far as it depends on you, live at peace with everyone" (Romans 12:18). It's not always possible to be at peace with another person amid conflict, because it takes two people with the same goal—healthy resolution. But as far as it depended on *me*, I would always strive for an equitable, respectful solution to any contentious issue.

A WELL-TIMED BREATHER

With those thoughts in mind, I suggested we all take a time-out, set aside time to consider the situation, and let emotions cool down.

For a couple of days, I wrestled with how to proceed. I knew that if we didn't resolve this conflict, it could undermine the project. I also realized I couldn't just brush it under the rug and hope it would go away. So I decided to take the initiative.

I asked Bruce to meet for lunch outside the office, hoping a neutral setting would help us talk more openly. When we sat down, I started by acknowledging how important the project was to both of us and how much I valued his expertise and perspective.

"Bruce," I began, "I want you to know how much I respect your opinion and your passion for this project. I've been thinking a lot about our last meeting, and I realize I might not have been as open to your ideas as I should have been."

Bruce looked at me, his expression softening slightly. "I appreciate you saying that, Dave. I've been thinking too. Maybe I was too focused on pushing my agenda without considering your concerns."

> Leaders should facilitate a process where all parties can voice their concerns, explore possible solutions, and agree on a way forward.

I nodded. "Obviously, we both care deeply about the success of this project, but we're coming at it from different angles. What I'd like to do is understand more about why you're so convinced that this aggressive strategy is the right move. I want to hear your reasoning, and maybe we can find a way to incorporate both of our perspectives."

Bruce sighed, leaning back in his chair. "Honestly, I'm worried that if we don't act now, we'll miss a big opportunity. The market is moving fast, and we need to be at the forefront of that change. But I also see where you're coming from—we can't afford a major failure right now. Maybe there's a way to test the waters without going all-in."

As we continued the conversation, something shifted. We both realized that our disagreement wasn't about who was right or wrong but about finding the best path forward for the company. By the end of lunch, we had reached a compromise: we would proceed with a scaled-down version of Bruce's strategy, allowing us to test the waters without fully committing to the higher-risk approach. This way, we could move forward with innovation while still managing the risks that concerned me.

What struck me most about that conversation was how much it deepened our relationship. By taking the time to listen to each other and address the conflict head-on, we not only resolved the issue but also built a stronger foundation of trust and mutual respect. The project, which I had once feared would be a source of ongoing tension, ended up being a success, and our team was stronger for it.

That experience taught me a valuable lesson about conflict resolution: it's not about winning or losing but about understanding and collaboration. By approaching conflicts with an open mind and a willingness to listen, we can turn challenges into opportunities for growth and strengthen our working relationships in the process.

CONFLICT CAN HARM OR HEAL

Conflict is an inevitable part of any workplace. No matter how harmonious a team may seem, differences in opinions, communication styles, and personal values will eventually lead to disagreements. As a leader, it's essential to recognize that conflict is not inherently negative; in fact, it can be a catalyst for growth, innovation, and stronger relationships if handled correctly. The key lies in resolving conflict in a healthy and constructive manner.

Once a conflict arises, it's crucial for leaders to act promptly and fairly. Delaying resolution can lead to resentment, decreased morale, and a toxic work environment. Leaders should facilitate a process where all parties can voice their concerns, explore possible solutions, and agree on a way forward. This might involve mediation, collaborative problem solving, or even bringing in an impartial third party to help guide the discussion. The goal is not to "win" the conflict but to reach a resolution that respects the needs and perspectives of everyone involved.

WHATEVER HAPPENED TO COMMON DECENCY?

It's not surprising that the American Bar Association's 2023 Survey of Civic Literacy began by saying, "Americans aren't very nice to each other anymore and they blame social media and the media generally." Findings included the following:

- 85 percent of survey respondents said civility in today's society is worse than it was ten years ago.
- 29 percent said social media is primarily responsible for eroding civility. Another 24 percent blamed the media generally, and 19 percent blamed public officials.
- 34 percent said family and friends are primarily responsible for improving civility in our society. Another 27 percent said it's primarily the responsibility of public officials, and 11 percent said community leaders.[15]

As a corporate leader for forty years, I have seen countless times how civility and healthy handling of conflict fosters a culture of mutual respect and kindness, promoting well-being and emotional resilience. Politeness and courtesy in interpersonal interactions contribute to a positive social climate, reducing stress and promoting psychological health. In contrast, a lack of civility can lead to increased levels of anxiety, aggression, and social isolation, undermining individual and collective well-being.

One study published in the *Journal of Occupational Health Psychology* found a link between toxicity in the workplace and symptoms of insomnia, a common symptom of clinical depression.[16] Other studies highlighted by the

Cognitive Institute demonstrated that incivility in the workplace leads to employee burnout, and rudeness in health care settings leads to diminished care and poorer outcomes among the ill.[17]

At the heart of civility lies a fundamental respect for others, regardless of differences in opinions, backgrounds, or beliefs. In a civil society, individuals engage in dialogue with a spirit of openness and receptivity, listening to diverse perspectives with honor and decency.

PRINCIPLES FOR POSITIVE DISAGREEMENTS

If you agree that some disagreements are inevitable in workplaces (as well as families and communities), then it's important to establish ground rules for healthy interactions. Start with these strategies:

Seek to understand what the conflict is really about. One of the first steps in addressing conflict is understanding its roots. Conflict often arises from misunderstandings, miscommunication, or unmet needs. It's important for leaders to approach each conflict with an open mind, seeking to understand the perspectives of all parties involved. This requires active listening, empathy, and a willingness to engage in difficult conversations. By taking the time to understand the underlying issues, leaders can address the real problem rather than just the symptoms.

Create a culture of open communication. When team members feel safe to express their concerns and opinions without fear of retribution, conflicts are more likely to be addressed early, before they escalate into larger issues. Leaders can foster this environment by modeling transparency, encouraging dialogue, and providing tools and training for effective communication.

Focus on the issue, not the individual. Personal attacks or assigning blame only serves to deepen divisions and make resolution more difficult. Leaders should encourage team members to discuss specific behaviors or situations rather than making generalized statements about a person's character. This helps to keep the conversation constructive and solution oriented. Any comment intended to demean or degrade the other person will do nothing to solve the problem or promote civility. It will only drive you and the other person further apart to say, "That's the stupidest thing I've ever heard!"

Use your ears more than your mouth. One of the principles in Steven Covey's popular book *Seven Habits of Highly Successful People* is this: seek first to understand rather than be understood. In the midst of a heated discussion, nothing facilitates progress as dramatically as listening. This can be tough to do when we're intent on defending our own position. But when we open ourselves to the other person's thoughts and feelings, barriers come down.

Make the goal of conflict unity and understanding. When two people encounter conflict, they stand at a fork in the road. One path leads to disunity and dissension; the other leads to unity and understanding. You can choose to fight mean and nasty, or you can choose to fight fair and open-mindedly. Each choice will reap consequences, either for loss or gain.

Ask questions first. Seek to understand the other person's perspective by asking thoughtful questions. If you don't understand what's being said or the motive behind the other person's perspective, ask for clarification. Sometimes it's helpful to restate what you heard the other person say to ensure that you interpreted their words correctly. After they finish speaking, follow up with, "What I hear you saying is ..."

Attend to tone. Have you ever had someone tell you, "I'm sorry," but know they didn't mean it? Even though their words communicated an apology, their tone sounded defiant and unapologetic. This is because the actual words we use account for only about 7 percent of how people interpret what we say, while tone counts for about 38 percent. That means our tone is about five times more important than what we say. So make sure you come across as genuine, regardless of what you have to say.

Call for a time-out. Once the fuse of anger is lit and tempers threaten to blow, the best bet is to create a safe space for yourself and others by walking away. The wisest action might be to say, "It seems like we're both getting fired up about this topic, so let's set it aside and move on." Let the other person know that you can come back to the discussion and face the issue at hand later—when you've both had a chance to calm down.

After a conflict is resolved, it's important for leaders to follow up and ensure that the solution is working and that relationships are being mended. Conflict can leave emotional scars, and it's the leader's role to ensure that the team heals and moves forward together. This might involve checking in with the individuals involved, providing additional support or resources, and reinforcing the values of respect and collaboration within the team.

While conflict in the workplace is inevitable, it doesn't have to be destructive. When handled with care, it can lead to deeper understanding, stronger relationships, and a more resilient team. Leaders play a crucial role in navigating conflicts, and by fostering a culture of open communication, addressing issues promptly and fairly, and focusing on solutions rather than blame, they can turn potential challenges into opportunities for growth and improvement. Healthy conflict resolution is not just about solving problems—it's about building a stronger, more cohesive team.

16

Keep Your Word

Sometimes integrity is inconvenient—
but it's always indispensable.

Most leaders would be quick to attest that they want
to be men and women of integrity. But you and I
both know that saying it is one thing, while living it can be
much tougher.

Nearly every day, situations arise that test our resolve
to live and lead with integrity. A tough PR situation might
tempt us to spin or misdirect information to protect our
reputation. An awkward personnel problem may coax us
to treat one person unfairly in favor of another. And who
among us has not sought to survive tough financial times
through a sudden turnabout in fiscal practices—even if such
changes renege on promises made during brighter days?

As leaders, our commitment to integrity can and will
be challenged daily. It sure was with my friend Keith, who
accepted a leadership position at a publishing company
only to find that he had inherited a prickly situation.

For years, Keith had successfully led teams in the book
publishing industry. A good chunk of his leadership experience was in the then-burgeoning Christian book niche,
where many executives, middle managers, and employees
were professing Christians themselves.

And Keith knew from experience that even Christian leaders who value integrity can lapse into compromise—purportedly to resolve a tense situation or "for the greater good."

WELCOME TO THE JOB

As the new VP of product development at Quantum Publishing, Keith's job was to lead a team of senior editors, contract specialists, and copy editors in the acquisition and development of eighty new books and ancillary products each fiscal year. Keith had been brought in to replace Tom, the former VP, who had led the product development division for four years.

Times were starting to get tough for the publishing industry in general. The U.S. economy had stumbled into recession, which accentuated several downward trends already at work within the book-buying market. Quantum had been unable to show a profit in the past two fiscal years—one reason why Tom was let go along with another VP. Now the company's board and CEO were yammering for a turnaround.

In Keith's first two weeks on the job, he assessed his inherited staff. All were talented, hardworking, loyal people. He spent additional time getting to know the four senior editors—Susanne, Jackie, Ted, and Derrick—because they were chiefly responsible for the quantity and quality of new book projects the company published each year.

THE "UH-OH" MOMENT

All four senior editors were on a salary-plus-bonus system that Quantum had put in place three years before. For a senior editor's bonus to kick in, he or she needed to acquire (contract) at least twenty new promising book projects during the fiscal year. A "promising" project was loosely defined as a book proposal that passed the muster of the publishing board, consisting of Keith, his senior editors, and the VPs of marketing, sales, and finance. For a book proposal to be accepted, all parties had to agree that its message and potential sales could reach or surpass minimum requirements for profitability.

The problem, Keith quickly realized, was that the current bonus plan seemed to have been hastily conceived; it did not take into account the bigger picture. The editors' incentive structure focused on their achieving the desired number of project acquisitions—which each senior editor had accomplished—but it failed to factor in actual sales and overall corporate fiscal health.

Keith flagged the bonus plan as something he'd revise for the coming fiscal year. But his senior editors now were due their bonuses for the *just-completed* fiscal year. The bonuses were to be paid within the next month, and the editors had all made plans for the bonus money they had earned.

THE CONFRONTATION

This was the issue that had just been tossed onto Keith's desk, as if it were the glove of a European dandy challenging him to a duel. In this instance, the dandy was Jason, the company's VP of finance, who sat across from Keith in Keith's office.

"It's just ridiculous," Jason said, his fist pounding the desk to emphasize his point. "We lose money again this year, but your senior editors still expect their bonuses.

We've *got* to stop this *ridiculous* payout when sales don't meet expectations."

Keith took a breath, trying to stay calm. This was only his third week, and here sat his peer from another division throwing down the gauntlet over a practice Keith had nothing to do with.

"Jason, I appreciate your pointing this out," he said, "because I'm still learning how things have been done here. My approach is to assess the present—thoroughly—before making changes for the future."

> Integrity is keeping an agreement even when the circumstances under which you made the agreement change.

"And the present isn't a pretty sight," Jason interrupted. "We're talking forty thousand. Forty thousand dollars in frivolous bonuses for your team—after another lousy year!"

Keith looked right at Jason, deliberately keeping his facial expression neutral. He prayed a quick, silent prayer for wisdom.

"Well, Jason, I'm all for tightening our belts, too, and I'll be doing whatever I can to help turn the bottom line around. But I've reviewed the bonus agreements that our senior editors worked under this past year. As far as I can tell, the bonus structure was agreed to by upper management, and it's based solely on reaching new-product acquisition goals—not on actual sales or corporate profitability. The editors' job was the acquisition of eighty new products, which is tough work. And they accomplished it."

Jason's face scrunched into a scowl. "But we hemorrhaged money last year, just like the year before. We had to let some people go. We delayed investment in facilities. We reduced some perks. It's just not right that *your* people receive large bonuses when we're trying to keep our heads above water."

THE NOT-SO-VEILED THREAT

Keith replied, "Jason, I'm not saying I would have structured the bonuses exactly as they were done in the past. In fact, I *will* assess and reconsider the plan as we move forward into this new fiscal year. But here's our situation now: The bonus agreement was for last fiscal year. The bonuses are *earned.* The editors worked their tails off and met their assigned goals. We owe them what was promised."

Jason wasn't moved. "*You* didn't make the promise. Tom did, and he's no longer sitting where you're sitting. Keith, you can come in here and make a *statement.* Show us you're here for the greater good. Take charge! No bonuses if the company isn't profitable. It only makes sense."

Keith took a long moment to absorb his colleague's challenge. Then, in a steady voice, he summarized Jason's challenge with a rhetorical question: "So go back on an agreement signed off by management a year ago—an agreement our employees fulfilled?"

"Tom made the agreement, not you," Jason repeated. "As the new guy, you can come in and make immediate changes for the better. Save a ton of money."

He rose to leave. Hand on the doorknob, Jason mumbled, "If you're set on proceeding with these bonuses, I might just bring Kevin into this."

Kevin was the company's CEO.

A not-so-subtle threat—after only two weeks on the job.

WHEN INTEGRITY MEETS REAL LIFE

Keith processed Jason's demand over the next several hours. Of course he wanted to get off to a good start in the eyes of his peers and his CEO. But he also wanted to earn and build the trust of his employees by delivering on what had been promised them a year before. Most important, one of his most important personal values was integrity, which calls for doing the right thing even when real life demands compromise.

The way Keith saw it, he'd inherited an awkward, prickly "trilemma" (a dilemma plus one). After pouring himself a fresh cup of coffee, he took pen to paper and contemplated three options.

OPTION A

In addition to your primary role of new-product VP, you are expected to help stop the corporate bleeding. Make an immediate positive impression on the CEO and your fellow VPs. Show them that you're decisive, you can be tough-minded, a company man committed to improving the bottom line. Gather your senior editors and explain, as gently as possible, that because it was a tough year for the company, it would be irresponsible to pay out the forty thousand dollars in bonuses.

OPTION B

Meet everyone halfway. Try to appease Jason, head off a potentially uncomfortable meeting with the CEO, and reduce the hit to the bottom line by adjusting (reducing) the bonus amounts. Gather the senior editors and explain that, because of the unprofitable year, it would be poor stewardship to pay the full bonuses. However, as a token of appreciation for your editors' hard work, you are happy to pay bonuses of five thousand dollars each, for a total of twenty thousand dollars, thus saving the company twenty thousand dollars.

OPTION C

Bite the bullet, endure some political and financial pain, and pay the bonuses in full. As a then-authorized agent of Quantum Publishing, your predecessor made a promissory agreement in the company's name. The bonus plan as written included no qualifiers making bonuses contingent on overall corporate performance. Therefore, the company should now meet its promissory obligation by paying the editors in full: ten thousand dollars each, for a total of forty thousand dollars.

THE PERSON [OR COMPANY] GOD BLESSES

So what was the right thing to do? As VP of finance, Keith's colleague, Jason, was paid to maintain a strictly financial perspective. But as VP of product development, should Keith's perspective be limited only to the numbers? He was dealing with hardworking, trusting *people*, not just with numbers.

What did personal integrity call for? Corporate integrity?

From somewhere deep in Keith's consciousness, a principle surfaced that he and some friends had discussed several weeks before at their monthly men's breakfast. The principle was from a psalm written by King David—timeless wisdom preserved over the centuries for days such as these.

In Psalm 15, the powerful king described the person God blesses. Among this person's character qualities, he or she is someone "who keeps an oath even when it hurts, and does not change their mind . . . . Whoever does these things will never be shaken" (Psalm 15:4–5).

> Maintaining integrity is not just a moral obligation for leaders; it is a strategic imperative.

Whoa. Keith looked up the verse on his phone, read it again, and the clouds began to part. On his yellow pad he wrote, "Integrity is keeping an agreement even when the circumstances under which you made the agreement change."

The person God blesses—the person of integrity—keeps a promise "even when it hurts" and does not change his mind. Integrity may require short-term cost or inconvenience, but it builds strength and stability for the long term—because colleagues and customers will want to keep doing business with you.

Keith paid the bonuses in full.

The VP of finance didn't like it.

Their CEO wasn't exactly delighted with it.

But if Keith was going to stand strong, he'd stand for integrity, not cancellation or compromise. He enabled Quantum to keep its word, even though it hurt fiscally. He maintained the trust of his editors, even though he had to face up to his peers and boss. But, promise kept, Keith assured his fellow leaders that he would institute a win-win redesign of the editors' compensation package for the coming fiscal year. A plan that everyone could live with.

Our guiding principle bears repeating: Integrity is keeping an agreement even when the circumstances under which you made the agreement change. Changing your mind midstream or after the fact is no longer an option.

Always keep your word. Not begrudgingly but cheerfully. In the future, make agreements carefully, then keep those agreements—*cheerfully*, regardless of what comes along. The trust and stability you build through uncompromising integrity will help elevate your entire enterprise.

And then, deep inside, you'll enjoy the peace of knowing you've done the right thing.

WHY INTEGRITY IS SO ESSENTIAL

Integrity is the cornerstone of effective leadership. It is the quality that builds trust, fosters respect, and establishes the moral foundation upon which all other leadership traits rest. In the complex and often challenging landscape of leadership, the temptation to compromise one's principles or to engage in deceitful practices can be strong. But maintaining integrity, even when faced with these temptations, is crucial for both the leader and the organization they represent.

Dozens of reasons exist for why leaders (and everyone) should maintain integrity, honesty, and unwavering moral principles. Let's focus on just a few of the top reasons.

First, integrity is vital because it builds trust. Trust is the currency of leadership; without it, leaders cannot effectively guide, influence, or inspire others. When leaders consistently act with integrity, they signal to their teams and stakeholders that they can be relied upon, even in difficult circumstances. This trust is not just about personal relationships; it extends to the organization's reputation. An organization led by individuals with integrity is more likely to be respected by customers, partners, and the broader community. This respect translates into long-term success, as people are more willing to do business with, work for, and invest in organizations they trust.

Second, maintaining integrity protects a leader's reputation and legacy. In today's world, where information is rapidly shared and scrutinized, even a single act of deceit can have lasting repercussions. Leaders who compromise their integrity for short-term gains often find that the benefits are fleeting, while the damage to their reputation is enduring. Once trust is broken, it is incredibly difficult to rebuild. On the other hand, leaders who remain steadfast in their commitment to honesty and ethical behavior leave a lasting legacy of credibility and respect. Their actions set a standard for others to follow and serve as a guiding example for future leaders.

Third, integrity is essential for creating a positive organizational culture. Leaders set the tone for the culture within their organizations. When leaders demonstrate integrity, they encourage their teams to do the same. This creates an environment where ethical behavior is the expected norm, where transparency and honesty are valued, and where people feel safe to speak the truth. In such cultures, employees are more engaged, more innovative, and more committed to the organization's goals. Conversely, when leaders are deceitful or compromise their principles, they may foster a toxic culture where dishonesty and unethical behavior are tolerated, leading to low morale, high turnover, and ultimately, organizational failure.

Fourth (and most important), maintaining integrity in a leadership role is not only a matter of personal and professional ethics but also a profound expression of faithfulness to God and adherence to biblical principles. The Bible consistently emphasizes the importance of honesty, righteousness, and justice—qualities that are foundational to integrity. Proverbs 10:9 tells us, "Whoever walks in integrity walks securely, but whoever takes crooked paths will be found out." This verse underscores that living and leading with integrity brings stability and security, both in our personal lives and in the organizations we lead. When leaders uphold integrity, they reflect God's character, embodying the truth, righteousness, and steadfastness that God calls his people to emulate.

What's more, maintaining integrity in leadership honors God by demonstrating obedience to his commandments. In Micah 6:8, we are reminded of what the Lord requires: "to act justly and to love mercy and to walk humbly with your God." Integrity in leadership means making decisions that align with these values, even when faced with challenges or temptations to do otherwise.

By leading with integrity, leaders not only set a godly example for those they influence, but they also invite God's blessings and guidance in their leadership. It is an act of worship and a testimony to God's transformative power, showing that his principles are not just ideals but practical truths that can guide every aspect of life, including leadership.

Maintaining integrity is not just a moral obligation for leaders; it is a strategic imperative. The pressures and temptations of leadership are real, but the long-term success of a leader and their organization depends on the leader's ability to remain true to their principles. By choosing integrity over deceit, leaders build trust, protect their reputation, and cultivate a positive organizational culture that drives sustainable success.

17

Give Them Wings by Giving Them Trust

Believe in your people—and they'll believe in you.

I'm convinced that my early years as an employee prepared me well for my subsequent years in leadership. In my early days I worked under both good and not-so-good managers. Okay, I'll speak more plainly, since I'm not naming names: I had some truly outstanding bosses and some truly lousy ones. More plainly: I had some gems and I had some jerks.

I personally felt both the positive and negative impact of their leadership style, and I also witnessed the results on my coworkers and overall team effectiveness.

I learned that one of the most fundamental components of good leadership is *trust*—trusting your team and demonstrating your trust daily. This applies to your team as a whole as well as to each individual.

And why not trust our people? We put enough faith in them to hire and train them. If we've trained and led them well, we should be confident of their "buy-in" to the mission. In my experience as both employee and leader, I've found that when a leader demonstrates trust in his or her employees, it boosts employees' confidence, motivation, and productivity. It certainly did with me as an employee, and I've also seen it lift the spirits of my people countless times.

Kristen was one of those people.

KRISTEN'S STORY

As one of my department leaders, Kristen was smart and diligent at her job. But during some especially intensive weeks, she seemed unusually frazzled and tired. When I asked her about it in our weekly check-in meeting, she responded with a weary smile.

"Well, Dave, to be honest, the special project I'm on has had its share of obstacles," Kristen said. "It's been one step forward, two steps back. I'm afraid I'm falling behind—not just on the project but on my regular duties."

We checked on progress to date, then explored some of the challenges Kristen was encountering. With me as a sounding board, she was able to come up with some new action steps, and I offered ideas of my own. Gradually, she seemed to relax and brighten.

As we wrapped our visit, I wanted to leave her with some sincere words of affirmation.

"Kristen," I began, "I've found you to be so good at your job, and so trustworthy, that I have full confidence in you on this project. Not only have you made progress, but you've skillfully handled some surprises along the way. I have absolutely no doubt about your wisdom and your ability to bring this in for us."

Until this moment, I'd never seen Kristen cry on the job. But I saw tears in her eyes as I expressed my trust in her. They were happy tears. She heaved a sigh of relief and blessed me with her beautiful smile.

"Thanks, boss," she said. "That means a lot to me—especially today."

"Oh, this is me thanking *you*," I replied. "Thank *you* for your good, hard work on this. You're a blessing to me, and I appreciate you so much."

I meant every word. Kristen left my office relieved and re-energized.

And she delivered for us—big-time!

I have found that demonstrating trust in my people leads to greater job satisfaction, higher productivity, improved morale, and better overall performance. When I consistently show confidence in my employees, it creates a positive work environment where team members feel valued and respected. *My boss trusts me. He trusts me to make good choices and do my job well.* This mind-set inspires higher levels of engagement and motivation, as people are more likely to go "above and beyond" in their roles when they feel trusted and empowered. *It feels good to be trusted. I'm not about to let my leader down.* Give your people wings, and they'll come through for you.

AVOID BEING A HELICOPTER BOSS

To give people wings, we need to steer clear of the morale-*busting* ramifications of an environment where trust is weak.

You've heard of "helicopter parents"—parents who may not fully trust their children or the people around them— who "hover" over their kids and their activities. While usually well-intentioned, helicopter parenting has proven to be both overprotective and overinvolved, robbing children of opportunities to socialize properly, to fend for themselves, to make decisions and learn from them. Without meaning to, helicopter parents can squelch their children's confidence and impede their growth to maturity.

Likewise, in the workplace, I believe there are "helicopter bosses," leaders who regularly overinvolve themselves. I worked for one in my early adulthood, and it wasn't enjoyable or empowering. He hovered over us. Micromanaged. Frequently questioned and countermanded our initiative. He was so consumed with overmanaging that he had neither time nor energy to focus on the bigger picture, as good leaders are supposed to do.

This man wasn't a people leader; he was a detail chaser. A hovering, annoying mother hen. The downdraft from his helicopter ways nearly flattened us into the ground. It left us almost paralyzed, fearful of venturing forth and doing the job with zeal.

> **If you overmanage and micromanage, you're only betraying your own self-doubt and insecurity.**

Then and there, I determined that I would never be a helicopter boss.

Lack of trust—even a *perceived* lack of trust—is like slow poison to a team's soul. It quickly metastasizes, diminishing morale and, inevitably, the quantity and quality of output. If you don't trust your people, I guarantee they won't trust you. They'll look on your hovering as a direct reflection of your own insecurities or inabilities. As Lao Tzu said in his classic book on military leadership *The Art of War*, "He who does not trust enough will not be trusted."

I'll be so bold as to state it this way: if you don't demonstrate trust, you're not a people leader; you're a helicopter boss. If you overmanage and micromanage, you're only betraying your own self-doubt and insecurity . . . and squandering your good people while you flounder.

That's why I've made the deliberate choice to lead people by providing calm guidance and then trusting them to do their jobs well. Instead of beating them down with helicopter downdraft, I've tried to give them wings.

THE HIGHEST HUMAN MOTIVATION

I agree with leadership expert Stephen R. Covey, who writes, "Trust is the highest form of human motivation. It brings out the very best in people."[18] Since you and I both want the very best from our people, today's the day to set aside any personal insecurities and begin improving our efforts to build them up. Today is the day to start demonstrating that we have full confidence in them to do their jobs with diligence, innovation, and excellence.

We empower people through our visible confidence that they know what they're doing and they'll do it well. We give them wings by lifting them up, trusting them, and providing encouragement and praise along the way.

GIVING THEM WINGS

To help you develop an environment in which trust and confidence thrive, I offer four principles that have proven successful for me.

1. Make trust your default attitude.

I made a point of telling my teams, "I want you to know that I trust you. You wouldn't be here if I didn't. I will keep on trusting you until or unless you show me that I shouldn't." Another way of saying this might be, "You don't have to *earn* my trust. I will trust you completely until you give me a reason not to."

This was not meant as a veiled threat but as assurance that I give people the benefit of the doubt from day one. I will trust and lead them with my full confidence in their ability and desire to do their jobs well. Trust is my default attitude toward them. It's only if someone drops the ball through negligence or halfhearted work, or exhibits a negative or contentious spirit, that I'll reevaluate my trust in that person and take appropriate action.

> We empower people through our visible confidence that they know what they're doing and they'll do it well.

Fortunately, I've had to take such action only a few times over the years. With trust as my default attitude, my people have responded by being increasingly trustworthy. Almost always, they've delivered for me—often above and beyond what I expected.

2. Give them guidance, then set them free.

Whether through the job description or a special assignment, it's vital that we give clear direction from the start. What's the task? What's expected? What does success look like? What boundaries need to be respected?

A friend of mine likes to tell his employees something like this: "Imagine a football field. Your job is to cross the goal line. But like a football field, you can't go out of bounds. For example, this ad campaign can't go beyond its established budget. Within the boundaries, though, you have the freedom to run this play or that play—your call—whatever produces a quality drive to the goal line."

My friend gives good guidance, then sets his people free to run. Or to fly. He refuses to micromanage. Instead, he stays apprised via weekly or biweekly touch-base meetings with his people to check progress, ask and field questions, and offer coaching and affirmation.

3. Express your full confidence—sincerely.

Remember my visit with Kristen, who was feeling beleaguered over a big project?

Our weekly check-in helped her unburden and see things more clearly. But after I sincerely expressed my respect and confidence in her, Kristen's countenance transformed from burden to buoyant, from overloaded to optimistic. She quickly regrouped and attacked the project with renewed vitality and creativity. Problems became mere speed bumps. And she came through for me and our company—above and beyond.

If you'd like to adapt my words to Kristen for your own use, go right ahead. Or you may want to use them as inspiration for your own. When you sincerely express and demonstrate your full confidence, you'll see a dramatic difference in your team's outlook.

4. Trust but verify.

I freely admit to borrowing this credo from Ronald Reagan, who popularized it while negotiating with Mikhail Gorbachev over nuclear arms reduction. For our purposes here, I borrow it for a very positive and constructive purpose.

Why trust but verify? Well, we're human. Once we determine to avoid looking over the shoulders of our good people, we could very easily *overreact* by making ourselves scarce. It's a balancing act. We want to trust and give our people wings, but it's also our job to stay apprised that the job is being done on time, on budget, and with excellence.

I've found the best setting for "trust but verify" is through weekly or biweekly one-on-one touch-base meetings, where your people can provide updates and consult you on challenges or next steps. You can ask clarifying questions, and they can ask theirs. You can coach gently, calmly, with words, tone of voice, facial expressions, and body language that convey trust.

This is verifying without micromanaging—staying informed without hovering. Your people are likely to leave their check-in meetings uplifted, because confidence breeds confidence. Your confidence enhances theirs.

18

See Everyone as Equal

Beware the pitfalls of playing favorites.

Early in my working life, years before I landed atop the corporate totem pole, I observed a common tendency among people who lead people.

I first noticed it after two or three of my colleagues would enthusiastically endorse our manager's viewpoint in meetings. Such would be followed by frequent casual chats between manager and said teammates, either at their doorways or in his office, sometimes with his door closed. After a few weeks, we couldn't help but notice that some of these employees were occasionally joining the boss for lunch at nearby eateries.

Eventually, as this trend continued, I noticed that morale and creativity seemed to be slipping among my other colleagues, and our workdays didn't seem as enjoyable as they used to be. I'm sure my teammates were wondering, as I was, about the apparent preferential treatment. Were these chosen few more important to the cause than we were—at least in the eyes of our boss?

Perhaps you've been on the receiving end of the unfortunate proclivity to play favorites—and you know how it makes people feel because you've felt it yourself. You've seen and experienced the damage left in its wake, as I have.

Once I became a leader, I resolved to ban any hint of favoritism from my management toolkit.

THE SUBTLE SLIDE

Unfortunately, it's way too easy for us to let some degree of favoritism take hold. Often we don't even realize it's happening. Robert Sutton, Stanford University professor and coauthor of *Scaling Up Excellence*, observes, "When it comes to playing favorites, no matter how fair you think you're being . . . you're probably guilty. Most of us are remarkably clueless about how we come across."[19]

> **The slide to favoritism is a subtle one.**

Granted, you will always have some employees who are easier to relate to than others. Perhaps they appear to work harder or care more deeply. They may also be easier to talk, laugh, and address problems with—more enjoyable to be around. In any group, such a spectrum in personal style is normal.

So the slide to favoritism is a subtle one. It may start as innocently as chatting casually with certain team members more often than with others. Next may come more frequent meetings in your office involving only the chosen few or more socializing during breaks or even at lunchtime. These employees may receive praise more often than the others or even the more desirable assignments. I've seen favoritism manifest in invitations to evening or weekend meals and fellowship in the boss's home. And even in selective enforcement where a favored employee gets away with policy infringements while other employees do not.

It doesn't take long for such partiality to be noticed by other team members, causing them to question their standing and value to you and to the team. Karen Dillon, author of the *Harvard Business Review Guide to Office Politics*, agrees, "With good

> Once I became a leader, I resolved to ban any hint of favoritism from my management toolbox.

reasons, you default to the people you consider to be excellent colleagues, the people you can rely on and enjoy. But when managers favor one employee over another, morale and productivity suffer. The danger is that you're laying a foundation for creating a dysfunctional team around you."[20]

Recently I came across a study that found that nearly 50 percent of American employees believe their managers play favorites, exhibiting "more praise, support, and socialization for some employees than others, giving some people more desired tasks, and excusing unproductive behaviors on a selective basis."[21]

It only slides downhill from there. The repercussions to your team and organization can be devastating: "Employees not only deemed favoritism as a form of workplace injustice/unfairness, but also reacted to favoritism behaviors with negative emotions toward the organization, less loyalty to the company, less job satisfaction, stronger intentions to quit the job, less work motivation, and more emotional exhaustion."[22]

So, as conscientious leaders, how can we avoid playing favorites—even the *perception* of playing favorites—among those who report to us?

EVERYONE COUNTS

A good starting point is to acknowledge multiple workplace studies revealing that men and women who *feel valued* are more likely to enjoy better physical and mental and emotional health and have higher levels of motivation, engagement, and job satisfaction. When employees are motivated, engaged, and happy, their attitude and their output are likely to show it.

So when it comes to leading your people, job one is to make sure that everyone on your team feels valued.

I suggest you keep a three-by-five card on your desk—where no one can see it but you—that reads "EVERYONE COUNTS." This is your reminder that it's your job to make sure everyone on your team not only *feels* valued but genuinely *is* valued. To that end, let me share nine simple (but pivotal!) practices to help ensure that "Everyone Counts."

1. Almost every day, find time to "manage by walking around."

Check in with team members one on one, starting with those who haven't recently had as much time with you as others. Use these "impromptu" visits to see how things are going for them—personally as well as job-wise. Don't rush; ask questions and truly listen. What do they enjoy most about their job? Are there obstacles that hinder their work? What could you do better to help them succeed? Try to check in with one or two team members each day and cover the whole team over a week's time. Then repeat the cycle diligently.

2. Make note of the names of spouses or significant others, outside interests, names and ages of children, or other information your employee may share with you.

Keeping this info in mind will help you make future "impromptu" visits more significant. On my teams, I found that an employee's eyes always seemed to brighten when I could ask how Jacob was doing in fourth grade or how young Monica did at her dance recital. Taking a moment to ask, listen, and comment on what people share goes a long way in building trust and rapport.

3. Seek opinions and feedback on work-related issues.

This can be especially effective in your one-on-one visits, as it demonstrates that you truly care about an individual team member's point of view. When asking for input during meetings, your most vocal people are likely to speak right up as always—but before you run with one of their opinions, be sure to ask the others what they think. I've been pleasantly surprised at how some of the wisest input will come from the "quiet ones" once they are personally invited to speak up.

4. Don't "block" others when they give input.

This should be a standing rule not only for yourself but for your whole team. To "block" someone is to dump cold water on an idea as soon as it's expressed. Common examples include the following:

- "We tried that before and . . . "
- "But . . ."
- "That wouldn't work because . . ."

You've likely encountered these and other blocks. You've probably uttered some yourself. If so, it's a habit I urge you and your team to break . . . and ban. If everyone counts, then everyone's *voice* counts. In our meetings we tried to counter the tendency to block by replacing "But" with "Yes, and." This small shift not only helped validate each idea, but it encouraged us to try to build on the idea.

With this discipline, we valued each person by seeking and affirming his or her opinion.

5. Praise often and publicly.
Catch people doing things right, and encourage the team to do the same with each other. When someone does something promptly and well, or a positive result is achieved, public praise is deserved and the person should be celebrated. But a caution: be sensitive to make sure praises are distributed as equally as possible. Those who plug away at less visible tasks are just as vital as the more visible or vocal folks.

6. Host "breakfast with the boss."
Have your assistant schedule a twice-yearly "breakfast with the boss" in which you invite two or three employees to breakfast (or lunch) with you. Again, start with those who may have received less of your time or attention lately; then schedule these meals so that each employee is included every six months or so. This is a great way to encourage both fun conversation as well as questions or issues your people may wish to bring up.

7. Respect the private hours.
Have you ever been on the receiving end of work-related calls, texts, or emails during evenings at home? On weekends? Or (perish the thought) on your vacation? Except for the very rarest of true emergencies, I believe that nothing at work is so urgent that it can't wait until my people are back at their stations and have had time to gear up mentally for their day. I encourage all managers and leaders to respect their people's personal time. They need it to rest, recover, and rejuvenate from the demands of your office and, most of all, to enjoy their private lives.

8. Be equitable with celebrations.

Friends in other organizations have shared with me how uncomfortable they were when some folks in the department received more elaborate birthday celebrations than others, or if someone's retirement was marked by a major party and a company-wide write-up while others' retirements were mere blips among their small team. Because everyone counts, I tasked my assistant with making sure all birthdays among my team were celebrated with equal verve and that other events received appropriate and equal commemoration. I also tried to have each employee's birthday on my own calendar so I could personally wish them the best on their special day.

9. Be careful when you share special values.

It's possible you share special values with one or more of your team members—political, philosophical, spiritual. If so, it's vital that you are extra careful about conveying even the appearance of special favor with these employees. In my case, as a devoted follower of Jesus Christ I never proselytized, but I also didn't keep my faith a secret. My employees knew where I stood, and we got along well. But I knew I had to be extra careful because a couple of other team members were Christ followers too. If I inadvertently showed any hint of special regard toward them, the others might think I favored them because they shared my beliefs. Not only could this reflect badly on our faith, but it also could create dissension among the team.

Everyone counts. Everyone. And because they count, they deserve to feel valued. If you keep yourself from playing favorites and put these ideas to work, you just may see your team flourish as never before.

19

Fail Forward

Turn setbacks into steps forward.

There's no getting around it: failures happen. And they can be painful.

Failures mean time, effort, and money spent and lost. They don't feel good. They can be embarrassing and might even become a black mark on your reputation on the job.

Like any CEO or team leader, I've experienced my share of initiatives that could have gone better. I've endured the disappointment and distress as a result, and I've helped dozens of my staff members work through the aftermath of their own failures.

I'll tell you about one of these failures in this chapter— not to wallow in mistakes my team and I made but to share how we were able to turn reversal into resilience.

And I'll assure you up front that failures are going to happen. If you've never failed, you're just not trying hard enough. You weren't hired to maintain inertia; you're there to move your enterprise forward. Growth requires risk. Nothing ventured, nothing gained.

Earlier in my career, I wrestled with how to respond to inevitable setbacks. But over time, I learned that failure can actually be an essential part of long-term success—when I face it boldly and follow up constructively.

"Knowing how to move on from failure is what can distinguish a successful person from others," writes Kevin Leyes, formerly of the Forbes Business Council. "A failed attempt does not make you a failed person; on the contrary, it makes you human. Accept the consequences and learn from them."[23]

Although it was challenging at times, I developed a new attitude toward failure that rarely let me down. I realized that every mistake or setback is a learning opportunity. We just need to make the best of it. Here's how . . .

FIX THE PROBLEM; DON'T AFFIX BLAME

While you may feel dismayed or upset over a failure, remember that your role as a leader is to exude steady, calm confidence. This helps reassure your team, who may be wondering if they'll be on the receiving end of a smackdown. And calm confidence is contagious. It says to the team, "We'll figure this out," and helps them believe it.

> Don't allow yourself or others to finger-point and dwell on the failure. You're there to fix the problem, not to place blame.

As soon as is practical, get together with those involved in the setback. This could be either individually, if the responsibility falls with one person, or as a group, meeting with all staff who played a role. You might say something like, "Let's take a close look at what's happened and see what we can learn from it." No hand-wringing or finger-pointing, just a coolheaded meeting invitation indicating that the situation needs to be fixed and you value their perspective on how to fix it.

My guiding principle for such meetings was that we were there to "fail forward." Since every mistake or setback is a learning opportunity, we want to leave the room upbeat and not beaten up, with two or three course-changing lessons learned.

I suggest you state this at the start of the session so that you and your people are focused not on "woe is us" or "who's to blame?" Your objective is to mitigate any damage, learn from the setback, and use it as a stepping stone to resilience.

In other words, you want to "fail forward."

IF YOU BLEW IT, OWN IT

I remember one situation in which I joined my marketing and sales teams to develop a special marketing emphasis that, we were convinced, would go gangbusters. It would require time, effort, and money, but we were all-in on the strategy.

Did it work? Um, not really. In fact, it bombed. Big-time.

I called a postmortem meeting and began with a sincere *mea culpa.* "I want to tell you all, I was as sold on this idea as you were," I said. "I gave the go-ahead, and I accept responsibility. But every setback is a learning opportunity, so let's put our heads together and figure out what went wrong."

In this and many other postmortems, I found that sincerely "owning" my own failure not only helped calm the situation but also conveyed assurance for others to think, *If my leader shows humility, so should I.* We were in this together. So together we performed a helpful postmortem and uncovered several good "lessons learned" as a result of the failure.

Even if you didn't personally play a part in the failure—if it's clear that one or more other team members are culpable for a setback—don't allow yourself or others to finger-point or dwell on the failure. You're there to fix the problem, not to place blame. And it's quite possible that the discussion may prompt any guilty parties to follow your example and fess up to their role in the situation.

DEFINE THE FAILURE

Next, I posed questions such as "Why didn't this work?" or "What did we miss?" You may have to call on someone to get the ball rolling. Then we brainstormed possible factors that may have contributed to the disappointing result. We had a team member take notes on a whiteboard so everyone could view key components of the discussion.

To wrap this part of the dialogue, I asked my participants to complete the following sentence:

This *mistake/attempt/strategic move resulted in disappointment because* _____ _____

_____.

There was more than one plausible answer, so we noted them all and sought consensus on the one or two most causative reasons for our failure.

"WHAT DAMAGES DO WE NEED TO MITIGATE?"

The failure you're dealing with may have required several staff to "drop everything" to invest inordinate time and effort toward the solution. Its poor ROI may have caused your budget and sales projections to take a hit. It might have also let down some customers, and even brought undue internal stresses during the development, rollout, and aftermath.

So now's the time to assess candidly any damages that may have surfaced from the failure. Take a deep breath, put on your humble hats, and note if and how your financials, customer relations, and internal relations may have suffered.

"WHAT CAN WE LEARN FROM THIS?"

Asking "What can we learn from this?" unlocks invaluable learning opportunities and almost always pulls helpful resolutions from the smoking ashes.

In our postmortem, one resolution we agreed on was this: "We will always test a strategy thoroughly to multiple market groups before expending the time and money to fully roll it out." Another was, "We will be sure to never overpromise a customer. Instead, we'll underpromise and overdeliver." You get the idea.

This, too, is a brainstorming exercise, so all opinions count and should be noted on the whiteboard. Later, participants refined their thoughts by identifying the two or three most compelling points.

"WHAT ACTION STEP(S) DO WE NEED TO TAKE NOW?"

This question gets your team thinking about how best to mitigate and rectify any damages the failure has caused. In other words, how best to "right the ship."

In our case, we determined that customers A, B, and C needed to receive conciliatory phone calls. We needed to recast sales projections and marketing plans. Our sales and marketing people decided to help compensate for the financial setback by shifting emphasis to a more proven product line over the next quarter.

Once we reached consensus on action steps needed, I assigned each action to individuals who held vested interest in making right the "wrongs" we had identified. Some actions may warrant your personal involvement as the leader; with one customer, I felt that I was the best and only person to make the contact to rebuild the customer's trust.

> Failures are opportunities to get up, dust yourselves off, and try again— a little smarter, a little wiser.

With assignments made, we set deadlines and a follow-up meeting one week later to update one another on steps taken and progress to date.

FROM REVERSAL TO RESILIENCE

Through this process, we were able to identify our mistakes, ease the damages, and regain lost ground—turning reversal into resilience.

There are invaluable lessons to be learned from failure. Properly implemented, those lessons will make you and your team better and stronger for the future. Bottom line, failures are opportunities to get up, dust yourselves off, and try again—a little smarter, a little wiser—to "fail forward."

20

Lean on Your Team Members

You don't have to be the smartest person in the room.

Early in my career, I came to a realization that would forever invigorate my leadership style. In fact, I made it a principle of leadership that I would try to implement whenever making major decisions affecting our people, our direction and strategy, or our big-picture vision.

Here's what I came to understand: even though I was the positional leader of my team or organization, I wasn't always the smartest person in the room. Nor did I really want to be.

Instead, the key to running a successful enterprise was to surround myself with good men and women who may have been more knowledgeable than I was in their respective fields . . . to empower them to speak up early and often as we solved problems or determined strategy or built vision . . . and to listen carefully and respectfully.

Quite often, my management teams contributed ideas or perspectives that hadn't yet occurred to me. Their seasoned experience in their areas of responsibility enriched our conversations, helped us "see around corners," and brought about better-informed outcomes.

I not only came to value their experience and wisdom; I sought it. I frequently gathered my management teams to help wrestle with big problems, adjust direction and strategy, and hammer out our corporate vision. As I sought and respected their perspectives, they in turn became confident that their opinions mattered. Together, more often than not, we landed on ideas and results far greater than I might have come up with by myself.

Management and group-dynamics experts refer to this phenomenon as *synergy*. I call it one of the most powerful, effective processes you can put to work as you lead your people.

COMBINED POWER

The Cambridge English Dictionary defines *synergy* as "the combined power of a group . . . when they are working together that is greater than the total power achieved by each working separately."

So synergy is when the end result is greater than the sum of its parts. One plus one plus one doesn't equal three; it equals ten. Sometimes even one hundred.

Here's how it typically worked for us.

Tom tosses out an initial idea. Sara says, "Yes, and . . . ," building on Tom's idea. Carlos pitches in with, "And what about . . . ?" Then Jack merges Carlos's contribution with Tom's and Sara's, which sparks a related idea. I summarize the discussion thus far, and we continue building. We may need to take what we have and live with it for a day or two; then we'll reconvene, reconsider, reconstruct.

At some point we'll ask, "But what if . . . ?" which challenges us to consider what might go wrong. So we work to storm-proof the ideas, solutions, or corporate vision we're talking about. Everyone is encouraged to contribute. No one gets blocked or put down. And the end result is far better than what we each contributed. One plus one plus one equals ten. Sometimes even one hundred! That's synergy.

There's no need to be a one-person show or a lone-ranger leader. If you and I aren't the smartest people in the room, so what? We've built a team of good people to help lead the enterprise. They're seasoned and they're street-smart. They *want* to help us better the cause.

So why not harness their exper-tise and desire? As leaders, why not

> *We* are usually smarter than *me*.

have the humility to acknowledge, as I heard one respected leader put it, that *"we* are usually smarter than *me."*

JUSTIN'S FOLLY: A CAUTIONARY TALE

To underscore this principle, let me tell you a cautionary tale—a sad but true story I heard from a friend.

A new leader had taken over my friend's department months before—a manager I'll call Justin. He mostly busied himself with day-to-day administrative work, rarely fully engaging in the bigger-picture aspects of leading the team. Often out of his office in meetings with higher-ups, Justin seemed distant, preoccupied with whatever his bosses were requiring of him. Over time, my friend and his coworkers began wondering among themselves, *Where are we going from here? Where does our department belong in the big scheme of things?* Questions any conscientious employee is entitled to ask.

Then, without warning, Justin suddenly sprang a vision statement upon his startled managers. My friend reported, "He called a management meeting, and there it was, on a big screen in PowerPoint for everyone to see, a detailed state-ment of how Justin envisioned our future as a department."

The managers' response was something all of us should learn from.

"When he finished reading his vision to us, the silence in the room was deafening," my friend said. "It's not that we disagreed with the vision statement itself, although there were obvious flaws. What caused our profound sense of underwhelm is the fact that it was *Justin's* vision and not ours. He had created it in a vacuum, with absolutely no collaboration with the stakeholders—all the leaders, managers, or others whose departments would be affected or impacted."

> **The key to running a successful enterprise was to surround myself with good men and women who may have been more knowledgeable than I was in their respective fields.**

In his attempt to be the smartest person in the room, Justin had run roughshod over his managerial team. He failed to take human nature into account—and failed to tap into the experience and insight his people could have brought to the table.

As James Kouzes and Barry Posner state in their book *A Leader's Legacy*, "Very few grown adults like to be told in so many words, 'Here is where we're going, so get on board with it.'" The authors go on to assert that people want to be part of the strategy- or vision-development process and that "it's the process and not just the vision that's critical in getting people all on the same page."[24] I agree. I've found that one's vision does not and cannot become team vision, or shared vision, if it's announced as though it were a revelation from God to a single enlightened individual.

Yet this was how Justin had come across to his managers. Not only had he ignored their expertise, but he had also failed to harness the power of synergy in what should have been a true team effort.

Let's see what happened in the wake of Justin's "revelation."

"Interestingly," my friend told me, "Justin's vision statement has not come up again since that surprise presentation last fall. Not once, from him or from us. No buy-in, no follow-through. We all suspect that he had sprung his vision statement on us in order to check off a particular task on his own upcoming annual review."

In other words, Justin's sudden outburst about vision not only dampened the morale of his people; it also was a complete waste of time.

"IF WE HAD HELPED BUILD IT . . ."

I hope that sharing Justin's folly—how *not* to inspire team members to move toward a shared vision—has simultaneously illustrated how problem solving, vision building, or strategic direction *should* be done.

Take special note of my friend's conclusion: "Had Justin conducted multiple work sessions with our team, we would have loved helping him develop an engaging vision statement of how we can best help the company thrive. More importantly, we would have been fully invested in that vision, 'bought in' from the start. No selling would have been required if we had helped build it."

Now, I may be a bit biased, but I think my wise friend should have been appointed as leader of his department. He knows what we're talking about. Justin, meanwhile, remains clueless.

We inspire vision by collaborating to make it the team's vision, not just our own. We solve big problems and determine strategic direction the same way. By recognizing that *we* are usually smarter than *me*, we can unleash the process and power of synergy . . . and bestow on our people the joy and dignity of collaborating toward *shared* vision. A vision that inspires and energizes the whole team.

21

Strive to Be Real and Relatable

*Leaders who use a personal touch bring
people together.*

I'll never forget the day I decided to bring my dog,
Stretch, to the Coinstar office. Stretch was a small white
terrier with a lot of energy, a perpetually wagging tail, and a
personality that could light up any room.

I had a big presentation planned—a company-wide
meeting where I would address the entire staff. Morale had
been a bit low, and I wanted to say something meaningful
that would bring people together. To be honest, I felt a
little nervous. I knew I had to connect with the team, but I
wondered how I could best make that connection.

It turned out that Nancy had gone out of town for a week
in New York City with her friends, leaving me in charge of
Stretch's pet care. He was a "people dog" who didn't like to
be left alone for long hours. So the day before my presentation, I asked my superb administrative assistant, Sister
Mary Darlene, if she thought it would be okay if I brought
Stretch into the office.

"Of course!" she said. "Our team will love him. And
besides, you're the boss, and you can do what you want.
Yes, the top boss should bring in the top dog!"

The next morning as I was getting ready for the day, Stretch kept following me around, tail wagging, as if he knew something special was about to happen.

"You're coming with me today, Stretch," I told him, as he cocked his head. "Your job is to make me look good and lighten the mood." With that, I grabbed his leash, and off we went.

> Leaders who lead with authenticity create a culture where employees feel comfortable being themselves, sharing ideas, and taking risks.

The moment I walked into the office with Stretch at my side, the atmosphere shifted. People were caught off guard in the best way. Smiles spread across faces, and a few chuckles followed us as we made our way through the building. By the time we reached the large meeting room for the presentation, I could feel the tension melting away.

I started the presentation with Stretch sitting on the stage as I stood at a podium. At first, he just looked out at the crowd with his signature head tilt, but soon enough he started wandering around, sniffing at chairs, and wagging his tail at people. Trying to give my quarterly updates, Stretch looked up at me, pumped up the cadence of his tail wagging, and let out a woof. The room filled with laughter, and suddenly, this wasn't just another dry corporate meeting. Everyone felt at ease.

As I continued speaking, Stretch kept stealing the show. At one point, he hopped onto a chair and sat there like he was an employee listening to my speech. The entire room broke out in laughter again. It was a lighthearted moment, but it created a deep connection between me and the team. They weren't just seeing their CEO—they were seeing someone who was human, real, and relatable.

What struck me most was how much more engaged people seemed that day. Usually, when I spoke at company-wide meetings, there was this layer of formality—people sitting stiffly, trying to decipher every word I said. But with Stretch by my side, that wall disappeared. We were all in this together, and the laughter and smiles in the room made me realize that people respond more to authenticity than they do to polished professionalism.

After the presentation, people gathered to talk—not just about the company updates but about Stretch. Some shared stories of their own pets, and others just thanked me for lightening the mood. That little terrier had brought us all closer, and in the process, I felt more connected to my team than I had in a long time. And I continued to bring Stretch into the office for a few hours every day that week.

Taking Stretch to work taught me a profound lesson about leadership. People don't just want a leader who's distant and polished—they want someone who is real and approachable. Stretch reminded me that sometimes all it takes is a little vulnerability and a lot of authenticity to build trust and connection with your team.

BREAK DOWN THE WALLS

In the world of leadership, there's often an unspoken expectation to maintain a level of professional distance, a façade of unshakable composure and infallibility. Leaders are expected to have the answers, project strength, and never let personal challenges interfere with their ability to lead. While this perception of leadership can create an aura of authority, it can also lead to disconnection, mistrust, and missed opportunities for deeper relationships with teams. The reality is, leaders who maintain professional distance and issue directives from the C-suites may earn respect, but they may also fail to inspire true loyalty and engagement.

In today's fast-paced and often turbulent world, people are looking for more than just competent leaders—they're seeking authentic leaders. Authentic leadership means being real, being human, and showing vulnerability when appropriate. It's about connecting with others on a deeper level, creating an atmosphere of trust, and building a team that sees you as more than just "the boss," but as someone who understands and values them.

THE POWER OF AUTHENTICITY

Being authentic doesn't mean abandoning professionalism or oversharing personal issues. It means being honest about who you are, letting your guard down when it's appropriate, and fostering open, genuine relationships with those you lead. People can easily sense when a leader is putting on a façade, and inauthentic leadership breeds mistrust and disengagement. But leaders who lead with authenticity create a culture where employees feel comfortable being themselves, sharing ideas, and taking risks.

Authentic leadership fosters trust, and trust is the foundation of any successful team. When leaders are honest about their challenges, when they admit mistakes, and when they show that they're still learning and growing, they model a culture of transparency and humility. This not only humanizes the leader but also empowers the team to bring their whole selves to work, to contribute enthusiastically, and to own their mistakes without fear of judgment.

CREATING A CULTURE OF TRUST

A leader's authenticity sets the tone for the entire organization. When you lead with authenticity, you create an atmosphere of trust and mutual respect. Employees feel more connected to leaders who are real, and that connection drives engagement, creativity, and commitment. When trust is high, employees are more likely to speak up, share ideas, and feel invested in the company's success.

Authenticity also enables leaders to be better listeners. When you're not preoccupied with maintaining a professional mask, you can engage in deeper, more meaningful conversations with your team. You become more attuned to their challenges, frustrations, and aspirations. This kind of connection builds trust over time and helps you lead with greater empathy and insight.

Trust, however, is fragile. If a leader is perceived as inauthentic or distant, that trust can quickly erode. By leading with openness and authenticity, you build the kind of relationships that withstand challenges and foster a loyal and committed team. People will go the extra mile for a leader they believe in, but they will disengage if they feel that leader is disconnected or disingenuous.

BALANCING AUTHENTICITY AND LEADERSHIP

Leading with authenticity doesn't mean baring your soul or sharing every personal detail of your life with your team. It's about knowing when and how to bring your authentic self to the forefront in ways that serve your leadership and your team. Leaders still need to provide direction, make tough decisions, and offer guidance. The key is doing so in a way that shows you're real and approachable, not perfect and aloof.

If your team is struggling through a tough project, being authentic might look like acknowledging the difficulty and empathizing with their challenges. It might involve sharing how you've faced similar struggles in the past and how you overcame them. It might also mean asking for input, admitting when you don't have all the answers, and creating a collaborative space where solutions can be developed together.

> **Authenticity allows leaders to connect on a deeper level with their teams, fostering trust, engagement, and loyalty.**

Authenticity doesn't mean lowering your standards or being overly casual; it means being genuine in your approach, building trust, and allowing your team to see you as a leader who cares about more than just results. When authenticity is balanced with clear leadership, it creates a powerful environment where both the leader and the team can thrive.

PRACTICAL STEPS TO LEAD WITH AUTHENTICITY

To close the distance between you and your team, and to be someone who leads with heart and soul, consider these strategies:

Be honest about your challenges. Don't be afraid to admit when things are difficult or when you're unsure of the best path forward. Let your team see that you're navigating challenges, too, and invite them to contribute to finding solutions.

Show empathy and care. Take the time to understand the challenges and concerns of your team members. Show genuine interest in their well-being, and listen to them without judgment.

Admit your mistakes. When you make a mistake, own it. Apologize when necessary, and share what you've learned from the experience. This not only models humility but also creates an environment where others feel safe to take risks and learn from their mistakes.

Share personal stories when appropriate. Don't be afraid to share personal anecdotes or experiences that relate to the challenges your team is facing. This can help humanize you and make you more relatable to your team.

Foster open communication. Encourage open dialogue and invite feedback. Create an atmosphere where your team feels comfortable sharing their thoughts and ideas without fear of judgment or retribution.

STRETCH AND THE HUMAN SIDE OF LEADERSHIP

A last note about Stretch . . . After I stopped bringing him into the office, all of our team members who attended our quarterly meetings seemed more interested in Stretch's well-being and hearing the latest stories than my reports about company numbers and progress. People would ask, "How's Stretch? What's he been up to? Has he gotten into any trouble lately?"

Because of the team's keen interest in that personable pooch, I started the meetings by giving a review and a story about Stretch to avoid the many queries about him in the question-and-answer period. Not surprisingly, when I decided to retire, the employees gave me a great party including many nice gifts for Stretch. He received a cool Harley-Davidson outfit complete with shirt, hat, and goggles (thankfully, no motorcycle). He wore his biker outfit with pride on many neighborhood walks.

Credit that terrific terrier for confirming a powerful principle for me: Leadership is not about being perfect—it's about being real. Authenticity allows leaders to connect on a deeper level with their teams, fostering trust, engagement, and loyalty. When leaders show their humanity, admit their vulnerabilities, and lead with empathy, they create an environment where both the leader and the team can grow together.

In a world where professional distance can often breed disconnection, the most impactful leaders are those who choose to be authentic, approachable, and human. It's through authenticity that leaders inspire others to follow—not because they're flawless but because they're real.

22

Find Strength in God's Faithfulness

Rely on God during difficult and daunting times.

I'll never forget the day it all came crashing down. For years, I had worked my way up the corporate ladder, leading several successful companies that were built on strong financial principles and trustworthy leadership. I had helped to lead those thriving businesses, and things were going well—until they weren't.

As I shared in chapter 5, during my time as COO at Paragon Trade Brands, a major lawsuit had been hanging over the company for months, a legal battle against a much larger corporation. I had faith that the facts were on our side, we would win the case, and everything would return to normal. But when the judgment came down, it wasn't in our favor.

The opposing corporation won, and the ruling was devastating. The financial penalties were astronomical—far more than I ever imagined we'd have to pay. In the blink of an eye, the company I had invested my life in was pushed to the brink of collapse.

The professional blow was hard enough, but the fallout didn't stop there. My personal finances were deeply tied to the company, and as we scrambled to figure out how to pay the settlement and cover our mounting legal fees, my personal savings, investments, and assets were all caught in the fallout.

The investments I had built over the years, the security I had provided for Nancy and myself—it all evaporated, leaving me on the verge of financial ruin. I couldn't believe it. Everything I had worked for, everything I had helped to build, was put in jeopardy in what felt like an instant.

When the legal judgment came down and the impact became clear, the first call I made was to Nancy, my lifelong anchor and encourager. I explained the legal judgment and its potential aftermath, even with the possibility of losing our home. No doubt as deeply alarmed and troubled as I was, she responded with her usual calm and comforting style.

"Dave, we've been through many ups and downs in the past," she assured me, "and we'll get through this one together. It will all be okay. I believe in you."

That is the kind of person you want to share life with!

The next "call" I made was to God as I prayed, *Help me, Lord, to walk through this terrible situation. Please come by my side to be my rock and fortress. Guide me as I try to honor all those who are affected by this very bad outcome.*

In the weeks that followed, the stress and heartache were overwhelming. I'd lie awake at night staring at the ceiling, wondering how it had come to this. I was a leader, someone others looked to for strength and answers, but I didn't have any for myself. I felt angry, embarrassed, and scared.

I held meetings with our entire workforce to explain what had happened and how they would be affected. They all trusted me to give them the unvarnished truth, and I did. Many of those on our team would face significant financial loss, and some would face the loss of their jobs. I did my best to project confidence and optimism.

One morning, in the midst of my despair, I found myself sitting in my living room with a cup of coffee, staring out the window, feeling completely lost. That's when something stirred inside me, a memory from my childhood—something my mother, a true saint, had always said when times were tough: "When you've got nothing left, you still have God."

I had always believed in God, but it had been years since I'd really leaned on my faith in that way. Sure, I prayed, went to church, and read the Bible, but I hadn't truly surrendered anything to God in a long time.

In that moment, I realized how much I needed to turn to him. I didn't have the answers, and clearly, I didn't have the control I once thought I did. But I had faith, and I knew God was still with me, even in the middle of this financial calamity.

I got on my knees right there in my living room. I prayed like I hadn't prayed in years—honestly, openly, laying all my fears, failures, and frustrations before God. I admitted I didn't know how to fix this, that I was scared of losing everything, and I asked him to guide me through it, to show me the way when I couldn't see one.

Over the next few months, things didn't magically get better overnight. The financial hardships were still there, the business still struggled, and I had to make some very tough decisions. But something changed in me. I felt a sense of peace and strength I hadn't felt before. I started to see that my identity wasn't tied to the success of my business or the size of my bank account. My worth was in God's hands, not the world's.

I also began to lean into the support of my Christian community. A few close friends became confidants during that time, offering spiritual guidance and reminding me that God often works through our deepest struggles to teach us reliance on him. Nancy and I prayed together regularly, growing deeper together in our trust in God. Our faith grew stronger as we walked through the uncertainty together.

Slowly, doors began to open. Opportunities I hadn't expected arose, and while I didn't regain everything I lost, I found new paths forward—both professionally and personally. But more than the financial recovery, what I gained was a deeper sense of trust in God. I realized that my security didn't come from the size of my portfolio, but from my relationship with him.

Looking back, I see how God carried me through the storm. The financial disaster I endured, triggered by a crushing legal defeat, caused plenty of sleepless nights and heartache. But it also brought me back to the foundation of my faith, teaching me that when everything else falls apart, God remains. And it's his strength, not mine, that ultimately sustains me through every trial.

RECOGNIZING OUR NEED FOR GOD

As leaders, we are often accustomed to being the ones who offer guidance, support, and solutions. We are the ones others look to for strength and direction, which can sometimes lead us to believe that we must always have everything under control. But the truth is, no matter how strong, capable, or prepared we are, there will always be times when we face situations beyond our capacity to handle alone.

Difficult seasons often serve as a reminder of our human limitations. In the face of overwhelming circumstances—whether it's a business failure, a personal loss, or a significant leadership challenge—it becomes clear that we cannot do it all. These moments strip away the illusion of self-sufficiency and remind us of our need for God. They invite us to humble ourselves and recognize that it is through God's power, not our own, that we can overcome trials and lead with grace.

In 2 Corinthians 12:9, the apostle Paul shares God's response to his pleas during a time of suffering: "My grace is sufficient for you, for my power is made perfect in weakness." This passage reminded me that it's not my strength, but God's, that matters most. In our weakest moments, God's power is revealed, and his grace carries us through. As leaders, acknowledging our need for God opens the door for him to work through us in ways we couldn't imagine.

> **Difficult and painful times will inevitably come, but they do not have to define our lives or our leadership.**

SURRENDERING CONTROL TO GOD'S PLAN

One of the hardest lessons for leaders to learn is the art of surrender. We're often trained to take charge, make decisions, and push forward, even when the road ahead is unclear. But faith requires us to do something counterintuitive: to let go of control and trust God's plan, even when we don't understand it.

During that painful time—and to this day—I relied on the words of Proverbs 3:5–6: "Trust in the LORD with all your heart and lean not on your own understanding; in all your ways submit to him, and he will make your paths straight." This Scripture challenges me to trust God fully, especially in difficult times when my own understanding fails me.

Surrendering control doesn't mean we stop leading or abandon our responsibilities. Rather, it means recognizing that we are not in control of the outcome. We can make decisions, take action, and do our best, but ultimately, we must trust God to guide us and work through the challenges we face. Trusting in God means believing that even in the pain and confusion, he has a purpose and plan for our lives and our leadership.

FINDING STRENGTH AND PEACE IN GOD

When trials come, it's easy to feel overwhelmed, anxious, or discouraged. Leaders may feel the weight of responsibility not just for themselves but for their teams, organizations, or communities. This pressure can be emotionally, mentally, and spiritually exhausting. But in these moments, God invites us to find rest and strength in him.

Isaiah 40:29–31 provides a powerful reminder of the strength that comes from relying on God: "He gives strength to the weary and increases the power of the weak. Even youths grow tired and weary, and young men stumble and fall; but those who hope in the LORD will renew their strength. They will soar on wings like eagles; they will run and not grow weary, they will walk and not be faint."

God doesn't expect us to carry the burdens of leadership on our own. He offers to exchange our weakness for his strength, our anxiety for his peace, and our weariness for his rest. In prayer and reflection, leaders can find the renewal they need to continue leading, even when the road is tough. When we anchor our hope in God, we find a strength that transcends our circumstances and a peace that surpasses understanding.

LEADING WITH FAITH THROUGH ADVERSITY

When leaders rely on God in difficult times, it not only transforms their personal journey—it also impacts the people they lead. Leadership during adversity is one of the most powerful witnesses to faith. When teams, organizations, or communities see a leader who remains steady, hopeful, and grounded in faith despite the challenges, it inspires others to trust in God's provision and presence as well.

A leader's faith in difficult times can be a source of encouragement for others. When employees, colleagues, or followers see that you are not shaken by hardship, they are more likely to remain hopeful and resilient themselves. Your ability to lean on God, to trust his plan, and to lead with courage and humility will ripple through your organization, fostering a culture of faith and perseverance.

Consider the story of Nehemiah, who faced tremendous opposition and challenges as he led the rebuilding of the walls of Jerusalem. Throughout the process, Nehemiah faced threats, discouragement, and overwhelming odds, yet he continually turned to God for strength, guidance, and protection. His reliance on God allowed him to lead with wisdom and determination, and ultimately, the walls were rebuilt.

As leaders, we also will face moments where everything seems to be working against us. But like Nehemiah, when we place our trust in God, we can find the courage to keep going, knowing that he is working behind the scenes for our good and his glory.

PRACTICAL STEPS FOR RELYING ON GOD AS A LEADER

Everyone has a unique spiritual path and practices to seek God's wisdom and direction. Here are some that I have found valuable as God walked me out of my darkest time:

Daily prayer and reflection. Make time for daily prayer and reflection, especially during challenging times. Lay your burdens before God and seek his guidance. Trust that he hears your prayers and is with you in every decision and circumstance.

Seek godly counsel. Surround yourself with mentors, spiritual advisors, or fellow believers who can offer godly wisdom and encouragement. God often speaks through others, and seeking counsel is a sign of wisdom, not weakness.

Surrender your plans. In difficult times, hold your plans loosely and submit them to God. Trust that he knows the bigger picture and is guiding your steps, even when the path isn't clear.

Focus on God's promises. Meditate on Scriptures that remind you of God's faithfulness, strength, and provision. His Word will anchor you in truth when your circumstances feel uncertain.

Lead by example. Let your faith be evident in how you lead during tough times. Be transparent about your reliance on God, and encourage your team or organization to trust in God's provision as well.

FAITH IN GOD GETS US THROUGH

Difficult and painful times will inevitably come, but they do not have to define our lives or our leadership. When we rely on God in the midst of adversity, we discover a deeper strength, peace, and resilience that comes only from him. As leaders, trusting God in our hardest moments allows us to lead with greater wisdom, humility, and compassion. It reminds us that our leadership is not about our own power, but about God working through us to accomplish his purposes.

> Surrendering control doesn't mean we stop leading or abandon our responsibilities. Rather, it means recognizing that we are not in control of the outcome.

In every season—whether in times of success or struggle—God is faithful. He promises to be with us, to guide us, and to strengthen us. As leaders, when we place our trust in him, we find that even the most challenging times can become opportunities for growth, transformation, and deeper connection with the one who ultimately holds our future.

Refocused, Not Retired

*True leaders don't stop—they shift their focus
to lead in different ways.*

It had been only a year since I'd retired, and I was still adjusting to the slower pace. After decades in the corporate world, the change felt jarring. I had gone from managing teams and making high-stakes decisions every day to suddenly having no urgent responsibilities.

At first, the freedom felt liberating. Nancy and I spent the winter in the California desert, enjoying time together, the warm weather, friends who visited, and countless games of golf.

But before long, I started to feel a little lost, like I had too much free time on my hands and no clear purpose.

Back in Seattle, Nancy and I attended a service one Sunday at our church, Bellevue Presbyterian Church. Afterward, I found myself talking to Pastor Scott Dudley. He'd always been someone I admired for his wisdom and perspective. We chatted for a bit about retirement life, and he invited me into his office to talk for a few minutes. There, I decided to ask him something that had been on my mind.

"Scott," I said, "I have enjoyed such a blessed life and a blessed career. But now I'm struggling to figure out what's next. I've spent my whole life leading teams, making decisions, and pushing forward in my career. Now that I'm retired, I feel like I've left all that behind. I mean, I love spending every minute I can with Nancy, and playing golf is fun, but I have much more to offer the world. Any thoughts to share with me?"

Pastor Scott gave me one of his thoughtful looks and then smiled. "You know, Dave, the Bible doesn't even mention retirement. Search

> "Your career may have ended, but your calling hasn't. The key is to keep serving with the gifts you've been given, just in different ways."

the Scriptures, and you'll never find a case of anyone retiring—at least not in the sense that we mean it today. In fact, the whole concept of retirement is pretty modern. People back then didn't stop working just because they reached a certain age. They might have shifted roles or responsibilities, but they kept contributing to their families, communities, and churches. The important thing wasn't stepping away from work—it was continuing to use their God-given talents."

That struck a chord. "So what does that mean for someone like me?"

"Well, think about it this way," Scott continued. "Just because you're retired from your corporate job doesn't mean your skills and experience are no longer valuable. I believe the restlessness you're feeling is God stirring your heart and soul. He has equipped you with leadership abilities, strategic thinking, and a lifetime of wisdom. There are so many ways you can still make an impact—whether that's mentoring young leaders, serving on nonprofit boards, or using your expertise to help people in need. The point is, you're not done yet, Dave. Retirement just means you get to use those gifts in new, meaningful ways."

I paused for a moment, letting Scott's words sink in. I had been thinking of retirement as a full stop, but maybe it was more like a comma—a shift, not an end.

Scott must have sensed my wheels turning, because he added, "This season of life can be one of your most impactful and influential, if you are open to following God's leading. Your career may have ended, but your calling hasn't. The key is to keep serving with the gifts you've been given, just in different ways."

That conversation stayed with me long after that Sunday. Scott was right—retirement didn't mean I'd spend my days playing golf and my nights watching TV with Nancy. No way. It meant I had the opportunity to use my experience in new, purposeful ways. And in that realization, I felt a renewed sense of direction, excited for what the next chapter might hold.

NEW BEGINNINGS

For many leaders, the thought of retirement brings a mix of emotions. After years of dedication, influence, and guiding teams to success, stepping away from the day-to-day responsibilities of leadership can feel daunting. But retirement isn't the end of influence—it's a new beginning. It offers a unique opportunity for reflection, renewal, and the chance to explore doors that have remained closed during the busy years of a career. For leaders who are accustomed to driving change and making impactful decisions, retirement can be the most liberating and fulfilling chapter yet.

The first step in seeing retirement as a time of opportunity is reframing the narrative. Instead of viewing it as a withdrawal from purpose, leaders can see retirement as an expansion of it. The years spent in leadership roles equip individuals with a wealth of knowledge, experience, and wisdom. These assets don't disappear upon retirement—rather, they can be used in new ways. Retired leaders often find that their accumulated skills are highly sought after in various fields, from mentoring and consulting to serving on boards and getting involved in philanthropy. The strategic insight and experience that took years to develop can be applied to new challenges and ventures that bring personal satisfaction and societal impact.

One of the greatest opportunities in retirement is the ability to mentor the next generation of leaders. For years, retired executives have honed the art of decision-making, risk management, and vision casting. These skills can now be shared with younger professionals who are just beginning their leadership journeys. Mentorship offers a way to stay connected to the business world while also contributing to the growth of others. It allows retired leaders to impart wisdom and guidance that can help others avoid common pitfalls and navigate their own paths to success. In this way, a leader's legacy continues to grow even beyond their formal career.

Retirement also opens doors for personal passions that may have been sidelined during the busy years of running a company or managing teams. Many leaders discover that retirement is the perfect time to pursue interests they never had time for in their professional lives. Whether it's traveling, writing a book, learning a new skill, or dedicating time to a charitable cause, retirement allows individuals the freedom to explore these passions without the constraints of a demanding schedule.

What's more, retirement presents the opportunity for leaders to reflect and redefine what success means. Throughout a career, success is often measured by tangible outcomes—revenue growth, organizational achievements, and career milestones. But in retirement, the metrics shift. Success becomes more about personal growth, relationships, and living with purpose. Retired leaders have the space to reflect on their experiences, make sense of their journey, and channel their energy into new goals.

Retirement brings the chance to create a balanced and meaningful lifestyle. Leaders who have spent decades in high-stakes roles often find that retirement is a time to prioritize personal relationships. Whether it's spending more time with family, reconnecting with old friends, or fostering new relationships, retirement allows for the cultivation of meaningful connections. This shift in focus brings an added dimension of fulfillment, as leaders now have the time and space to invest in the people who matter most to them.

MY NEXT STEPS

After my conversation with Pastor Scott in his office, and several more that followed, he asked me to help the church leadership with issues they were struggling with. I stepped in on numerous occasions to help with tricky personnel problems, leadership development among the staff and volunteers, vision brainstorming for future growth, and other situations that tapped into my experience.

Those opportunities sparked an idea, and I began offering my guidance to many other churches and non-profits, serving along with a friend who had also retired after years in management positions. In most of these situations, the top leaders were highly skilled in a specific area but not trained to oversee large organizations and teams.

It was a privilege to come alongside scores of leaders who were struggling or needing fresh ideas.

Eventually, Scott suggested I talk to Brent Christie, who was leading Jubilee Reach, a nonprofit in Bellevue, Washington, that had been founded by our church a few years before.

Around this time, Scott preached a sermon on how to determine if you are being called by God to pursue a new direction. Scott said if you feel you are being called by God, just take one step and then determine if it's a real call. Right then, I decided to talk with Brent to see if I could serve him.

> Instead of viewing it as a withdrawal from purpose, leaders can see retirement as an expansion of it.

As we were leaving church, Brent was blocking our path. I walked up to him, introduced myself, and asked if I could be of any service to Jubilee Reach. He immediately said yes and asked me to meet him in his office on Monday morning at eight.

The next morning, we had a wonderful three-hour meeting. Most of it was Brent telling me about his challenges and opportunities. I had some questions, but most of the time I tried to absorb what he was telling me and understand how I might be able to serve him and the ministry.

I learned that Jubilee Reach is a nonprofit organization dedicated to serving struggling youth and underprivileged individuals in the Bellevue area, providing a wide range of support services for those facing economic hardship, academic challenges, and social isolation. At the heart of Jubilee Reach's work is a deep commitment to empowering youth. Many young people who come from difficult backgrounds face a range of barriers that hinder their academic progress and personal development. Jubilee

Reach addresses these challenges by offering after-school programs, tutoring, and mentorship designed to help students not only succeed in school but also develop life skills and self-confidence. The organization works closely with local schools to identify at-risk youth and provide the individualized support they need to thrive.

In addition to its focus on youth, Jubilee Reach serves underprivileged individuals and families through a variety of community outreach programs. From providing food and essential household items to offering job training and adult education classes, the organization helps lift people out of poverty by addressing both immediate needs and long-term self-sufficiency.

I was very impressed with the belief that this was a ministry of Christ and we didn't own it, but it was our responsibility to show the love of Jesus to hurting, needy people in our community. As we ended the meeting, Brent mentioned that my contribution might be to help him and his small team focus on the most important issues. We agreed on that, and I focused on that for the six years we worked together. We agreed to meet every Monday at 8:00 a.m., and I became Brent's helper, encourager, and advisor.

Besides helping Brent, Scott thought I should become the Jubilee Reach chairman of the board. Because of all of the challenges I'd had with the Coinstar board, I declined, wanting no part of board work for the first year of my retirement. But eventually I felt God's calling to move into that leadership role and served there for many years.

I have felt immensely privileged to contribute and help guide Jubilee Reach into a period of significant growth with many new initiatives for serving thousands of people.

As I learned, retirement is not the closing of a door but the opening of many. For leaders, it marks the beginning of a new chapter filled with fresh opportunities to mentor, explore personal passions, give back, and live a more balanced life. It's a time for reflection, renewal, and rediscovery.

Rather than a retreat from influence, retirement is an opportunity to continue making an impact, but on one's own terms. With the right mind-set, it can be the most exciting and rewarding phase of life—a time when new adventures await and doors open that were previously unseen.

Notes

1 M. Scott Peck, *The Road Less Traveled* (New York: Simon & Schuster, 1978), 65.
2 "Optimism and Your Health," Harvard Health Publishing, May 1, 2008, https://www.health.harvard.edu/heart-health/optimism-and-your-health.
3 Alan Rozanski et al., "Association of Optimism with Cardiovascular Events and All-Cause Mortality," JAMA Network, September 27, 2019, https://jamanetwork.com/journals/jamanetworkopen/fullarticle/2752100.
4 Rosalba Hernandez et al., "Optimism and Cardiovascular Health: Multi-Ethnic Study of Atherosclerosis," National Library of Medicine, 2015, *Heath Behavior and Policy Review*, 2(1), 62–73, https://doi.org/10.14485/HBPR.2.1.6, https://www.ncbi.nlm.nih.gov/pmc/articles/PMC4509598/.
5 Eric S. Kim et al., "Optimism and Cause-Specific Mortality: A Prospective Cohort Study," 2017, *American Journal of Epidemiology*, 185:1, 21–29, https://doi.org/10.1093/aje/kww182, https://academic.oup.com/aje/article/185/1/21/2631298.
6 Eric S. Kim et al., "Optimism and Cause-Specific Mortality: A Prospective Cohort Study."
7 Robert Intrieri and Paige Goodwin, "The Life Orientation Test: A Confirmatory Factor Analysis Across Three Age Groups," National Library of Medicine, 2020, *Innovation in Aging*, 4(Suppl 1), 459, https://doi.org/10.1093/geroni/igaa057.1486, https://pmc.ncbi.nlm.nih.gov/articles/PMC7741639/.
8 Rezan Nehir Mavioğlu, Dorret I. Boomsma, and Meike Bartels, "Causes of Individual Differences in Adolescent Optimism: A Study in Dutch Twins and Their Siblings," Springer Nature Link, 2015, *European Child and Adolescent Psychiatry* 24, 1381–388, https://link.springer.com/article/10.1007/s00787-015-0680-x.
9 Guido Alessandri et al., "Much More Than Model Fitting? Evidence for the Heritability of Method Effect Associated with Positively Worded Items of the Life Orientation Test Revised," 2010, *Multidisciplinary Journal*, 17(4), 642–53, https://doi.org/10.1080/10705511.2010.510064, https://www.tandfonline.com/doi/abs/10.1080/10705511.2010.510064.
10 https://pubmed.ncbi.nlm.nih.gov/21450262.
11 David B. Daniel, "The Impact of Recognition and Praise on Employee Engagement and Motivation," *International Journal of Business Management*, 2013.

NOTES

12 Christina L. Kammeyer-Mueller and Jeffrey A. LePine, "Employee Recognition and Its Impact on Employee Motivation and Job Satisfaction," *Journal of Applied Psychology*, 2016.

13 Adam Grant, *Give and Take: A Revolutionary Approach to Success* (New York: Penguin Books, 2014), 157.

14 Dale Benson, *The Leadership Lectures: Practical Wisdom for Health Care Leaders, Managers, and Supervisors*, 2nd ed. (2017: Leadership Development Institute, 2023).

15 "ABA Survey: Civility Is Vanishing—And It's the Media's Fault," AmericanBar.org, April 27, 2023, https://www.americanbar.org/news/abanews/aba-news-archives/2023/04/aba-survey-civic-literacy/.

16 Caitlin A. Demsky, Charlotte Fritz, Leslie B. Hammer, Anne E. Black, "Workplace Incivility and Employee Sleep: The Role of Rumination and Recovery Experiences," 2019, *Journal of Occupational Health Psychology*, 24(2):228–40, doi:10.1037/ocp0000116, https://pubmed.ncbi.nlm.nih.gov/29683714/.

17 Lynne McKinlay, "The Importance of Civility in Preventing Burnoout," Cognitive Institute, accessed October 28, 2024, https://www.cognitiveinstitute.org/preventing-burnout/.

18 Stephen R. Covey, *The 7 Habits of Highly Effective People: Powerful Lessons in Personal Change Interactive Edition* (Mango Media, 2016).

19 Rebecca Knight, "How Managers Can Avoid Playing Favorites," *Harvard Business Review*, March 15, 2017.

20 Rebecca Knight, "How Managers Can Avoid Playing Favorites."

21 Victor Lipman, "Does Management Play Favorites?" *Psychology Today*, October 26, 2021, https://www.psychologytoday.com/gb/blog/mind-the-manager/202110/does-management-play-favorites.

22 Victor Lipman, "Does Management Play Favorites?"

23 Kevin Leyes, "Five Tips on Turning Failure Into Success," Forbes.com, September 14, 2020, https://www.forbes.com/sites/forbesbusinesscouncil/2020/09/14/five-tips-on-turning-failure-into-success.

24 James Kouzes and Barry Posner, *A Leader's Legacy* (Hoboken, NJ: John Wiley & Sons, 2006), 56.

About the Authors

Dave Cole is a seasoned business innovator and corporate leader with over forty years of experience leading some of the world's top companies. Starting his career in sales with Procter and Gamble, Dave moved on to hold senior leadership positions at Quaker Oats Company, Cadbury Candy Company, Weyerhaeuser Industries, Coinstar, and other prominent organizations. Known for his visionary leadership and ability to drive growth across diverse industries, Dave has made a lasting impact in the corporate world.

After transitioning from corporate life, Dave chose not to retire but instead redirected his focus toward giving back to the community. He became a key leader at Jubilee Reach, a Bellevue, Washington, nonprofit organization dedicated to serving underprivileged youth and families, where he has, for twenty years, channeled his expertise and passion into making a difference in the lives of others. Dave's commitment to service reflects his belief in the power of leadership both in business and beyond.

Dave summarizes his life and career as the story of how a modestly gifted man achieved significant success in a very difficult and challenging world, with help from a gracious God, a wonderful wife, and fabulous friends and colleagues.

Dave and his wife, Nancy, reside in Seattle, where they enjoy being involved at their church, volunteering, mentoring, and golfing.

Keith Wall, a thirty-year publishing veteran, is an award-winning author, magazine editor, radio scriptwriter, and online columnist. He currently writes full-time in collaboration with numerous best-selling authors. Keith lives in a mountaintop cabin near Manitou Springs, Colorado.